WILLIE KNOWS WHO DONE IT

WILLIE KNOWS WHO DONE IT

Reports from the Byways of Maine

Hans Krichels

atmosphere press

TABLE OF CONTENTS

PART I –
FROM HERE TO YUCCA FLAT
AND OTHER STORIES

(Note: I came to Maine almost fifty years ago. If I ask an old-timer if he's lived here all his life, he will drawl, "Not yet." He will tell me I'm not a real Mainer. I will ask him if my kids, born in Bangor, are real Mainers. He will point out, "Iff'n my cat has kittens in the oven, that don't make them muffins, now, do it?" This morning, I am gathering a small collection of tongue-in-cheek stories, for the most part, poking fun at all of us that live up here – and anywhere else, for that matter. In later chapters, I'll share more serious material, even some story-poems, as I call them.)

THE BATTLE OF THE TITANS

The outlook wasn't brilliant for the hippie team that day. The score stood 3 - 1 with half an inning left to play. With Wilson safe on first and Skeegan huggin' third, a pall-like silence fell upon the patrons of the game.

And that's how it is as our story unfolds – Jillian, fearsome Jillian at the bat, everyone holding their breath, anxious. Despite all disclaimers, this was a showdown, a battle of the titans between the Blueberry Barons (aka the Outback Nine) and the Milltown Maulers.

This all happened back in 1975 in a little town called Bridgeport up there in Maine on the banks of the mighty Penobscot River. Bridgeport at the time was a mill town basically, with its huge paper mill, though lots of teachers and artists, retired folk, and commuters to other communities lived there too. By 1975, there was also a fairly substantial contingent of newcomers, out-of-staters, back-to-the-landers, homesteaders, hippies, some called them, who had bought up land in the outer reaches of the township. Rumors, misunderstandings, stereotypes ran rampant on both sides, and something called The Green Grass Softball League provided something of a common ground for the various factions.

In the days before the homesteaders, the good folks of Bridgeport had organized the League as part of summer programming in town. Teams sprang up with names like The River Sharks, The Main Street Merchants, The Milltown Maulers, The Dairy Porters, The Pulp Beaters, The Bakers' Dozen, and others. Some of these teams had rivalries beyond the ball field, but not one of them was fully prepared for a new team that sprouted up at the time of

3

this story – a team calling itself the Blueberry Barons.

As I said, rumors abounded on both sides. Whisperings amongst the townsfolk: Did you know that marijuana was being grown in a clearing out by Hancock Pond? Processed and sold by long-haired strangers to innocent children on playgrounds around town? That "Viva" on a tee-shirt was a slogan of subversives and communists? Or, from the other side, that you had to be careful walking down certain roads at night; shots would be fired. Rednecks roamed the byways looking for longhairs to gun down. And forget about trying to get credit at the bank – or even fair return on that rotten board you got at Old Henry's sawmill out by the lake.

There was an evening back then – and this was a year or so before the great Green Grass showdown we're talking about. The newcomers, perhaps a dozen households scattered though the valleys and hillsides, all "homesteaders" in one way or another, some of them doctors, lawyers, teachers, from "away" and some of them collegiate athletes a few years back, had developed a tradition of sorts – Thursday Night Revels, it was called. Every week, weather permitting, they would gather in a clearing in the woods up on something called Whitetail Ridge. A small bonfire lay at the heart of the festivities. Foods were cooked, salads shared. And, yes, there was homebrew and probably the occasional marijuana joint being passed around. By ten most families had gone home and tucked in for the night. But on this particular Thursday night, just after nightfall, there was the sound of a truck making its way up the rutted road to the ridgetop. A hush fell over the revelers, a shiver of anxiety.

The truck ground to a halt and sat there idling for a

long minute before a grizzled, wiry man emerged and, staggering a little, approached the revelers. By the dome light behind him could be seen a woman and three or four small children in the cab of the truck.

"I'm here to get my daughter," the man announced. "Sally. She run off with the hippies. I need to talk to your leader." The man was slurring, obviously drunk, obviously terrified. Backed up by his family in the truck and a good deal of liquid courage, he was confronting the abductors of his missing daughter.

"I need to talk to your leader," he repeated, and finally a man stepped forward and explained that there was no leader, just a group of friends getting together for a cookout. "You're welcome to join us," he added.

"I need to know who beat up my daughter," the man said. Did he mean beat up – or knocked-up?

A woman, Jillian, tall and decisive, stepped forward, talked softly to the man, explained that there was no Sally at the party. She took the man by the elbow and guided him back to his truck. He appeared to be sobbing as he climbed into the cab and drove his family back down the ridge road.

In the discussion that followed, all agreed that the poor guy's daughter had probably gotten pregnant and run off with some high school sweetheart. And everyone marveled at the courage it took, fortified or otherwise, for the grieving father to pack his family into the truck and confront the dope-crazed, Sally-abducting hippies dancing naked on Whitetail Ridge in the moonlight.

Yes, they marveled. And they talked deep into the night, as children fell asleep around the fire. And in the morning, a small contingent appeared at the Town Recreation Department and signed a new team up for the Green Grass

Softball League; it would be called the Blueberry Barons.

In the months that followed, it would be nice to say that friendships were formed, misunderstandings corrected, that teamwork and camaraderie prevailed. And while that was all true, to a certain degree at least, a subtle rivalry persisted. And while the Blueberry Barons gained a certain amount of respect – they had some highly skilled players – they lost most of their games. Rarely could they assemble a full team for game day, and there were huge gaps around second base and in the outfield. Add to that a feeling more ambassadorial than competitive, a certain reluctance to actually outscore their opponents.

Meanwhile, back on Whitetail Ridge, Jillian was putting the finishing touches on a goat barn she'd been building. In addition to playing oboe in the off-season for the Cleveland Symphony Orchestra, she was a skilled gardener and carpenter. More to the point of this story, Jillian had captained, batted clean-up, and won the national championship with the Villanova Women's softball team. In fact it was Jillian who secured that championship with a long bases-loaded home run in the bottom of the last inning. Now, as she hammered a board into place on her goat barn, Jillian was feeling a bit resentful that the "boys," such as they were, had been prioritizing green grass softball as the activity of the season. She looked at the dismal record of the Blueberry Barons and decided it was time for her to take charge of the situation.

It was in early August that Jillian was officially added to the roster of the Blueberry Barons. To say that turmoil ensued would be to overstate the case. But there was a lot of confusion and blustery chivalry. Some teams refused to play the Barons altogether; some argued that it just wasn't right; others claimed that they were just afraid of hurting a girl, hitting her *there*, as they called it. And some teams would come and play the game but refuse to pitch to Jillian or slide in to second base. There was no overt animosity, just a lot of discomfort and glancing away.

Until one day, that is, it was decided in certain quarters that enough was enough. One team in particular, the Milltown Maulers, reached the breaking point. There would be no more tiptoeing around (*Pussyfooting around*, their first baseman chortled, *Beating around the bush,* leered their catcher). It was time to face the problem squarely. They would play the Blueberry Barons; they would pull no punches this time around, and they would kick butt once and for all. Their centerfielder, tall and wiry, a recent addition to the team, did not participate in the discussion.

The day of the game dawned misty and cool. By evening, the sun was shining brightly, and a substantial crowd had gathered at the Green Grass ball field. Friendly greetings abounded, and a disputed call in the early innings was settled in favor of the Barons – upon unanimous insistence by the Maulers. This would be a *fair* game, if nothing else. And, when, following a three-run homer by the Mauler centerfielder, Jillian lofted a solo home run of her own late in the fourth inning, there was cheering from all sides. Still... especially as the seventh and final inning approached, an ill-defined tension settled over the bleachers. For all the goodwill in the world, all the insistence that this was just a game, for all of that and deep in the hearts of both sides, this game *mattered*.

And so, it all came down to this – bottom of the final inning, Maulers up 3-1, two outs, runners on base and

Jillian, elbow scraped and pant leg torn from a vicious slide into second, stepped from the dugout.

There was ease in Jillian's manner as she stepped up to the plate, a certain pride in her bearing, a smile playing on her lips. The crowd fell silent. The pitcher, a stocky young man from the night shift at the mill, tipped his hat to the crowd and pawed at the ground.

Strike one whistled past. Jillian crowded the plate. Ball one. Then ball two. Then ball three, high and outside. Strike two just caught the inside corner, brushing Jillian back. She glared disapprovingly before lofting the next pitch deep into centerfield.

Deep, deep went the ball. Back, back raced the centerfielder. Wilson was already rounding second, Skeegan holding at third. The ball sailed deeper, centerfielder racing back, back, leaping high over the fence, snatching the ball like a fly out of the blue summer sky and waving it high for all to see.

The crowd, stunned for a moment, gasped. Some groaned; most cheered at the phenomenal feat of athleticism.

The centerfielder walked to the infield, removed her ball cap, shook down long tresses and smiled radiantly at the crowd. She and Jillian embraced briefly and bowed in all directions.

From his truck, just beyond the outfield fence, a grizzled, wiry man, alert, happy, and sober at last, smiled and waved to his daughter. "Proud'a you, Sally," he called out. The scoreboard read Maulers 3, Barons 1, but that is not what the crowd remembered from that day.

THE PRINTS AND THE PAUPER

Bradbury was tired of being poor. Even old Henry up the road wasn't poor – not the way Bradbury was poor, subsisting as he did on cucumbers and the dwindling hope that one of these days he would snare some protein from the forest. Bradbury wasn't exactly envious of the old man – but, dammit, for Henry, always grinning and puttering around, the whole business of survival seemed so, well, *incidental*. And dammit again, Bradbury had more going for himself than the old man had ever had. In fact, the more Bradbury thought about it, the more it struck him that poverty, for him at least, was inexcusable. "No point a smart feller like you scratchin' around like an old banty-hen," Henry himself had said that very morning. Face it, the old man was right.

Bradbury surveyed his options. He was twenty-seven years old, after all, and, yes, he was tired of being poor. Employment, of course, was out of the question. Bradbury had decided *that* years ago – which was why he was poor in the first place. Gang activities, bank-heisting included, were also out of the question. Ethical considerations aside, very much aside, Bradbury was not a group-joining person. What he needed was a one-man operation, a low-risk, high-yield, solo enterprise. Counterfeiting, for example, was not out of the question. Bradbury lived in the country, in a log cabin built over an old cellar hole. The cellar hole was perfect for clandestine operations. There was even a natural safe of sorts – a large cavity behind a squared-off, pink granite rock. He could keep his operation small, specialize in one denomination, twenty dollar bills, say, crisp new twenty dollar bills by the armload. Of course, Old

9

Henry, always stopping by, snooping around, would wonder, think he was pushing dope – or, worse, inheriting money. By Henry's ethic, at least you had to work at pushing dope.

Bradbury rejected the counterfeiting scheme as too risky – and not just because of Old Henry. Computerized supermarkets alone left him reeling; visions of the modern crime lab were more than he could handle. Besides, triggered by the thought of Henry, another idea had come to him, something more within the range of conventional business ethics – not to mention his own skills and inclinations. He spent the rest of the evening recalling stories the old man had told him, tales of the old days, of wildlife that once roamed the forests, of cougars in particular, of a time or two when townspeople locked their doors and windows.

Bradbury pondered into the wee hours of the night, mulling and scheming. By morning, he was ready for action. He fired off a letter to a friend in New Mexico, requesting four items in particular – and a small loan, just to tide him over. Then he buried himself in the stacks of his local library. By the end of the day, he was something of an expert on the subject of turn-of-the-century local wildlife – on the subject of cougars in particular. He returned to his cabin with a legal pad full of notes and a book on a not altogether different subject under his arm. The book was called *Safari*, and it included a chapter on chemical big-game repellants.

That all took place on a Monday. On Tuesday afternoon, Bradbury returned *Safari* to the library and sent a carefully-worded letter to Chemco, Inc. in Cincinnati, Ohio. The rest of the week he spent organizing his wildlife notes, waiting, refining his strategy. Except for afternoons, which he spent weeding his cucumbers and checking his rabbit snares. The rabbit snares were invariably empty; witch grass had invaded the cucumbers. Bradbury slept feverishly these days, consumed by plotting and dreams of the future.

The following Monday, there was a package for Bradbury at the post office. *Jack's Taxidermy / Albuquerque, New Mexico,* read the label. Bradbury bought four toilet plungers at the hardware store and headed for home.

"Four cougar paws," read the note inside the package. "As requested. Numbered counter-clockwise from right front to right rear. What are you up to now, Bradbury ol' buddy? You owe me big time." Bradbury squinted at the message in the dim candlelight of the old cellar hole; there was a check for five hundred dollars attached. Bradbury folded the check neatly into his pocket and held the paws, one by one, up to the flickering light of the candle. Perfect: Jack was the best; he'd pay him back double when his ship came in. Bradbury spent the rest of the afternoon setting the paws, like large, padded jewels, into the cups of the toilet plungers. Then, counter-clockwise, from right front to right rear, one through four, he notched the handles of the plungers; he would have to be able to tell in the dark.

Bradbury was whittling his last notch when three long blasts of a horn flushed him from his cellar hole. Blinking in the sunlight, he signed the release and helped the UPS driver unload the truck – carton after carton, forty-eight in all, from Chemco, Inc. in Cincinnati, Ohio. It was well after sunset before Bradbury found himself, secure in his cellar hole once again, perched on his inventory and scanning his

11

contract with Chemco. "Exclusive regional dealership..." He liked that. "Product: Bwana: Big Game Repellent." Bradbury suspected that Bwana was nothing more than repackaged Mace, but no matter: it was the packaging that counted. He glanced at his plungers and nodded his head. He would begin at daybreak.

With Tuesday's dawning, Bradbury was up and stumbling through the puckerbrush, clutching by its handle a guitar case full of toilet plungers. By sunrise, he had found what he was looking for – a soft, oozing spot of ground, just firm enough to hold an impression. He selected his #2 plunger, a left forepaw, from the guitar case. Angling the plunger in accordance with his wildlife studies, he pressed a single print into the mud and returned the plunger to its case. He was home in time for breakfast, a long morning nap, and an afternoon of anticipation. As usual, his rabbit snares were empty; his cucumbers were succumbing to the witch grass.

With the coming of evening, Bradbury was back at his mudhole. An eager child was with him, one of Henry's innumerable grandurchins, his bicycle parked nearby. Bradbury pointed to the paw print, traced its outline with his finger, told the child he should ask his grandfather about it. The child raced away on his bicycle. Bradbury wondered if the old man would take the bait.

For three days, Bradbury wondered and waited. By Friday afternoon, he knew he was in business. A picture appeared in the local weekly: old Henry stood beside the mudhole, pointing at the paw print. A uniformed game warden stood beside him, and the grandurchin hovered in the background. The picture was accompanied by a short article: old Henry hadn't seen a cougar in these parts in fifty years, it said. The game warden agreed, speculated a bit, emphasized the harmless, reclusive nature of the big cats.

Bradbury was off and running. Ten miles to the north, the *Big City Daily* picked up the story. The cat, so to speak, was out of the bag. It was time now to thicken the plot.

Discreetly now, by the light of the night sky and the nine lives of his Eveready batteries, Bradbury began to roam the countryside. Plunger #1, Plunger #2, Plunger #3, Plunger #4—he used them all, not randomly or indiscriminately, but sometimes in combination and always with attention to the minutest of details.

Night after night, Bradbury plied his trade. In time, he grew accustomed to the newspaper accounts. "More tracks found ... outskirts of town ... circling ... growing bolder..." By the end of the second week, Bradbury detected the first hints of hysteria in the accounts. He laid a final set of tracks at the Big City limits and temporarily retired his plungers. Shortly thereafter, he appeared at the editorial offices of the *Big City Daily* with a manila envelope under his arm.

Bradbury's article was a scholarly work, deeply rooted in his studies of turn-of-the-century wildlife, of cougars in particular, in the newspaper's circulation area. It detailed the history and habits of the big cats; it emphasized their harmless, reclusive nature; it scoffed at attacks on humans and family pets. The clinical, detailed descriptions of these attacks, discounted as they were, fit nicely with the scholarly tone of the article. The editors were impressed and paid him well. Bradbury returned home whistling. He stashed his first profits behind the pink granite rock in the old cellar hole. Bradbury was pleased – but far from finished.

In the days – rather, the nights – that followed,

Bradbury resumed his print-making efforts. With the waning of the moon, he grew bolder, crossing forbidden boundaries, penetrating town limits, plunging, as it were, into the unknown. Flower gardens, vegetable gardens, parks and pastures – nothing, at least no spot of ground soft enough to hold an impression, was sacred. And then, without even waiting to gauge the reaction, Bradbury retired his plungers again and launched the second phase of his operation.

"Bwana," Bradbury told the buyer at the hardware store. "From Chemco, Inc. in Cincinnati, specialists in big-game repellants."

"Bwana," he told the man at the drugstore. "Twelve dollars a can." He rented a van, trucked his stock to the Big City and sold Bwana by the boxload. By mid-afternoon, he was sold out. He placed a collect call to Chemco, Inc. and spent the rest of the week taking orders. His business was growing by leaps and bounds; he loved every minute of it.

And so it went, week after week through the summer. Bradbury's cucumbers gave way altogether to the witch grass; his rabbit snares went unchecked. By late summer, Bradbury's cellar wall safe was overflowing; he would have to do something about the safe, invest the money somewhere, buy into Chemco, maybe...

Oddly, it was on the very evening that Bradbury first had trouble fitting the pink granite rock back into its niche that old Henry came by for a visit.

"Howdy, Brad."

"Been a long time, Henry."

"Business goin' pretty good?"

"Couldn't be better, Henry."

"You was pretty quick on your feet with that Bwana

stuff there. Good thing a man knows how t'grab a opportunity."

They sat on Bradbury's doorstep. "Yep," old Henry continued, "it's a real good thing." He paused and spat a stream of tobacco juice. "Funny thing, too. Old Witt Bowden – use t'live here, just like you – made hisself a pile of money off'n the cougar, too. Raised a cub. Use t'charge folks a quarter t'come see it. Kept the money b'hind a rock in the cellar. Pink rock granite, I b'lieve t'was."

Old Henry chuckled, and Bradbury cringed a little at the shrewdness in his eyes. "What came of it all?" he asked, but the old man ignored him.

"Lordy," Henry continued, "Witt use t'mistreat that cat somethin' awful. Kept him half-starved – so's he'd be fierce for the customers, y'know. Well sir, one day Witt Bowden went just a little bit too far. That old cat busted clean outa his cage and lit into Witt like the divil hisself. Weren't nothin' left but bones and a belt buckle."

Again, old Henry paused, spat tobacco. "Folks say that cat musta lifted the latch hisself. Lotta talk in them days. Folks talkin' about the cat comin' back, too. His spirit, y'know, hauntin' the place. That's how come they burned the old place down. Folks just tryin t'pertect themselves, y'know..."

Again, Bradbury was aware of the old man watching him shrewdly. Neither one of them mentioned the remarkable cougar coincidence – or Witt Bowden's stash of quarters, for that matter.

That night, Bradbury slept badly, haunted by visions of gleamings in the darkness – belt buckles, shiny quarters, slit-eyes shining, shifting, twinkling from old Henry's sockets.

In the morning, the grandurchin reappeared on Bradbury's doorstep. "Grampa said t'give you this." He handed Bradbury something, a gleaming belt buckle. "He thought you might want it. Sorta like a souvenir, he said."

Bradbury clutched the gift in the palm of his hand. The child sped away on his bicycle. Bradbury's knuckles whitened. By midday, his fingers were numb, and, by late afternoon, he had hiked far up the road and tossed the buckle into the back of a passing truck. That night, he did not sleep at all.

With the coming of day, Bradbury lay twisted in his blankets, listening apprehensively, struggling to distinguish between dream and reality. Something seemed to be thumping on the door below. Bradbury shivered. At last, slinking and peering about, he approached the door and opened it a crack. The grandurchin had returned. "Wanna show you something, mister," he said.

Bradbury hesitated. Then, reluctantly, he dressed and followed the child, followed like a puppy to his original mudhole, the site of his earliest efforts. There, he watched the child park his bicycle and point to something: a large paw print in the mud. "Fresh," the child said, tracing the outline with his finger.

"Naw," scoffed Bradbury. Wearily, he recalled that the print couldn't be fresh; he hadn't plunged in the mudhole since his very first outing. No doubt about it – they were looking at the original paw print - Plunger #2, left forepaw, perhaps somewhat enlarged and altered by the rain, but remarkably well-preserved. No doubt at all. None, whatsoever. Still, Bradbury gave the child a quarter and told him to keep his mouth shut.

Moonlight found Bradbury back at the mudhole,

Plunger #2 in one hand, his Eveready, flickering through its ninth life, in the other. Heart pounding, Bradbury fitted his plunger to the paw print ... and fell back groaning. It was like fitting a child's foot to a man's shoe – and Plunger #2 to a Plunger #4 pawprint, to boot. Bradbury crouched by his mudhole, groaning and struggling to gather his wits.

Perhaps it was the lack of sleep. Perhaps it was the cumulative stress of his business ventures. Perhaps it was simply the mysterious matters at hand. Whatever it was, Bradbury did not gather his wits. Midnight found him at the gates of the State Hospital, guitar case in hand, begging for asylum. Daybreak did not find him: Bradbury was in a windowless, padded cell, riding his plungers like pogo sticks, hooting and raving at the walls.

But daybreak did find old Henry. He was whistling his way homeward. In one hand, he carried a bulging satchel; in the other – Henry, lover as he was of all things wild and wonderful, had not, on this or any other day, neglected to check Bradbury's snares – a large and meaty rabbit. Henry was whistling at the thought of the tangy and tasty stew that simmered in his immediate future.

As for Bradbury, he was never heard from again. Folks say it's a shame: he never did experience the pleasure of an old-time rabbit stew.

As for a moral to the story, let it be this: a fool and his bunny are soon parted.

[Originally published in KENNEBEC — A Portfolio of Maine Writing, Augusta, Maine]

THAT OLD
BABCOCK ROAD MISERY

Billy Hyde-Bunker changed his name after his divorce. Cindy Hyde-Bunker had grown tired of country living, had grown tired of Billy's deep, philosophical ruminations, and had run off with Billy's old college roommate, a successful lawyer down in Boston. Following this best legal advice, Cindy took her old surname, Bunker, with her into her new life. Billy was left with just Billy Hyde and the hyphen.

Billy was not exactly devastated. He had always been on one quest or another, and his current situation wasn't much different. After many days of soul-searching and wandering around the countryside, Billy decided to ditch the Billy Hyde part of his name altogether. Something deep inside him sought closure, anonymity. He kept only the hyphen. Now he called himself "-", short for hyphen. He changed his name officially, and he came to be known as that around the countryside – this lonely figure wandering the byways, doing odd-jobs for folks occasionally, playing a little harmonica he carried in his hip pocket. People pronounced it differently, but that was what he was known as: "-".

No one knew for sure where "-" was actually living at that point. His old homestead was gone, lost in the divorce. When a sheriff's deputy came by one day, intent on "serving papers", as he called it, "-" was nowhere to be found – no mailing address, no listing in the phone book. Google searches for "-" found no one going by that name. If not a man without a country, he was a man without a street address, at least.

Or so it appeared to old friends and countryfolk alike -

not to mention the stout sheriff's deputy. At the same time, certain old friends would later recall that Billy, as he was back then, may have been quirky and lost in thought, never easy to figure out, but he was also not without skills and resources. Reports began to circulate: folks along a certain stretch of unpaved road were hearing muffled sounds of hammering and sawing from deep in the woods, along with sightings at times of a dilapidated pick-up truck with expired license plates and a bed full of timbers and cedar shakes. Some folks even claimed to have seen the truck disappear behind a thick stand of hemlock along the old Babcock Road *over t'the Corners*, before rumbling off into the woods. No one by the name of "-" was on file at The Registry of Motor Vehicles. But "-" was there somewhere, it was said on the grapevine, up the old tote road *off'n the Babcock Road*. And "-" *was* up to something.

Yes, definitely, a man not without certain skills and resources. In his years as Billy Hyde-Bunker, Billy had been known as an excellent carpenter, a thinker, a poet, a man who read widely and advocated for the rights of indigenous peoples. The words of one wise Chief in particular stuck with him: *Man cannot own the land upon which the people walk.* "-" (Billy at the time) had taken that to heart. Friends and neighbors all around him were acquiring land, calling themselves back-to-the-landers, joining homesteading movements and land trusts. But not Billy; he was gradually divesting himself of belongings and properties, including sweet, charming Cindy, loved and admired by all. Something in Billy at that time was yearning to be free, whatever *that* was. He found himself nodding along as he read Melville's story of Bartleby the Scrivener. It was at that time that he heard of something else, too – something that

19

resonated deeply – an idea, yes, but something real, too - something called a *misery*, a particular misery in the case at hand.

A misery, as Billy came to understand, was a small unclaimed piece of land – a country without a man, such as it was. In the early days of surveying the land, he was told, the surveyors would start at one point and mark off the properties one by one. Occasionally, when they reached the end of a particular stretch of road, there would be a little piece of land left over. This little piece of land would be referred to as a *misery*. In the particular case along Babcock Road, the little misery was about twelve acres and accessible only via an overgrown and abandoned tote road, hidden behind a stand of hemlock, just down the hill from Sammy Hutchinson's place.

In his old life as Billy, "-" had become fascinated by the idea. The thought of vanishing, of living in obscurity on a piece of no man's land called a misery, captivated him altogether. "No man is an island," John Donne had thundered from his pulpit all those centuries ago, but Billy had set out to prove him wrong. Now, as "-", just "-", he charted his course accordingly. Beyond his truck and a few tools of his trade, he would own nothing; he would live off the grid. If not exactly Henry David of Walden Pond, he would be "-" of Babcock Road Misery.

In the days, weeks, and months following his official divorce, "-" became increasingly entrenched in his new digs. The cabin he built for himself was secure and dry and warm on chilly nights. His old truck gave up its ghost, and he abandoned it behind the barn at Sammy Hutchinson's place. When the deputy from town, still hoping to serve papers, finally discovered the truck, Sammy blustered and professed ignorance. "-" was an old friend of his, and he could count on Sammy to keep his secret. He could also count on Sammy for occasional trips into town for groceries and essential supplies. Beyond that, "-" did everything in his power to create a state of non-existence for himself. It was not oblivion that he sought; there were simpler ways to achieve that. His goal, simply enough, was to make no tracks, to leave no trace.

How "-"'s existence – or non-existence as he preferred - came to be known beyond his little corner of the world is anyone's guess. Perhaps he shouldn't have been quite so chatty and forthcoming with that nice saleslady at the hardware store. On his solitary, contemplative walks through the forest, he had distilled a pretty concise and poetic statement of purpose for himself – for himself alone, he would insist, though it amazed him how lightly it tripped off his tongue, how nice it was to watch that saleslady's eyes light up as he told it. Was it his fault if she wrote down what he was saying? How was he, in his trackless isolation to know what transpired on social media in those days? How was he to know that his trusted friend Sammy, known in the past to be less than discreet with lady friends and bedmates, was engaged in a deep and sharing relationship with this lady, Maggie was her name, at the hardware store? How was he to know that this story of a man named after a hyphen in a name, living in a hideaway on a piece of land owned by no one, living a virtually trackless existence would become an object of such fascination to trekkers and seekers, to young people all over the world?

It wasn't long after that that the first seekers showed up at "-"'s hideaway. Any irritation he felt at the intrusion was quickly overridden by the shining eyes of his acolytes, their eager scribbling in little spiral notebooks, as pearls of wisdom fell from his lips. When they left, "-" would go back to his job of doing nothing, leaving no trace, and, oh yes, distilling his thoughts into pithy sayings and haiku for his visitors – should they ever return to his doorstep.

And return to his doorstep, they did, old disciples and new converts as well. The untracked little path to "-"'s hideaway became something of a highway. Unknown to "-", little books began to appear, the scribbling of his disciples. A magazine editor showed up, took several pictures, and made an appointment to return for an interview. There was talk of a movie, a documentary. It was all a little overwhelming. His very state of non-being, so essential to himself, so intriguing to the world-at-large, was under siege. And this was only the beginning.

Confused by it all, "-" hiked up the hill for consultation with his old friend Sammy. *Relax,* Sammy told him. Homebrew was carefully poured into a growler. A business partnership ensued. Sammy would take care of the business, be an agent of sorts. Access to the misery would be controlled. A bank account would be set up in the name of "-," just "-".

And so it came to pass. The fame of "-" grew by jingles and koans. Months, maybe a year went by. "-" declined an invitation to appear on the Oprah Winfrey show.

It was then that the stout deputy returned and knocked at "-"'s door with considerable authority. Henry Hawkins, it said on his name tag. He was serving papers, as he explained it. Two sets of papers in fact, actions being initiated by Cindy, under the urgent advising of her lawyer. The first set of papers, ancient history by now, sought to regain partial custody of the hyphen she had abandoned so blithely. And now a new set of papers. Cindy's lawyer had become aware of "-"'s new bank account, bursting with deposits from royalties, crowd sourcing initiatives, donations; his fan club was wealthy and worldwide by now. Cindy was contesting not just ownership of the hyphen but, by extension, ownership of the huge bank account as well.

"-" watched the broad back of the deputy disappear down his trail through the woods. He felt sick to his stomach at first. Then again, he thought, he *was* feeling a bit overwhelmed by it all. Face it. What the heck, he was ready for a new chapter in his life anyway. That night, he hiked up the hill to Sammy Henderson's place. Homebrew flowed. *What the heck*, "-" kept saying. Sammy posted the words on the official Facebook page, and young people around the world began greeting each other with *What the heck*. It was translated into eighty-seven different languages and printed on fourteen million T-shirts.

The following night, back at Sammy's place again, "-" abandoned himself to an impulse and placed a call to Boston.

"What say, Cindy? You feelin' like me? Maybe this whole thing...we made a mistake?"

He shifted to speaker-phone, and he and Sammy listened together to the enthusiasm in Cindy's voice. Yes! A mistake had been made. That's exactly what she'd been thinking. She was tired to death of Pete and his legalisms; she'd totally underestimated "-"'s capabilities. A mistake had most definitely been made. However... And here she paused. "-" and Sammy groaned inwardly and held their breath. However, she repeated, it wasn't the mistake "-" was thinking of. Cindy herself hadn't been a business major in college for nothing, after all. This "-" bullshit could be branded. She saw huge potential here, great new markets to develop, a retreat center to be cashed in on. She would drop her silly lawsuits, of course, and they would take it from there. She could see it now: "-" as Spiritual Director, she herself as Director of Operations, Sammy and (what was her name, Maggie?) as Business Managers. Oh, she could see it now: the Babcock Road Misery Retreat Center, complete with bungalows, pavilions, and meditation centers—not to mention a little gatehouse out by the old Babcock Road.

And so it came to pass — a scene just a few years later: bungalows and lean-tos nestled under the cedars, a pavilion under the whispering hemlocks with seekers by the score mesmerized on their prayer mats, gazing adoringly as "-" speaks from his podium. In a cabin nearby, Cindy and Sammy and Maggie keep the books and schedule future events.

Meanwhile, out in the gatekeeper's lodge, just beyond the cedars, a certain Hank Hawkins, recently retired from the County Sheriff's Department, keeps track of the comings and goings. His uniform is starchy with an official logo on the breast — "-" in bright colors. Underneath, he wears a T-shirt: *What the Heck* it reads across the stoutness of his belly.

THE CURIOUS INCIDENT
OF THE MAN IN THE FOG

Fog lay over the river that morning; shadowy figures passed outside as Mayor Bill Keeney, recently voted to head the Town Council, shuffled papers at his desk and gazed out his window. A soft knocking came at the streetside door. Bill Keeney pressed a button on his desk, and a buzzer sounded. Muffled footsteps in the hallway. A long pause. Bill Keeeney listened attentively. The footsteps continued; a figure entered the office and stood facing Bill Keeney - a smallish figure, a woman with sharp features and a look of disbelief, even disgust, on her face.

"So I see you've removed the plaque," the woman said. Her face was half-hidden by a cowl; her voice was grave, a bit raspy around the edges.

Bill Keeney shrugged. "Folks don't care any more," he said. "Most folks don't even know what it's all about."

The woman across from him shook her head slowly and shoved hands deeper into pockets. 'There are those of us," the voice was and deep and sonorous now, "who do care. Who care very much." With that, the woman turned, walked down the hallway, and disappeared once again into the fog. Outside, visitors to the Town Offices noticed a particularly tapered footprint in the soft soil around the petunias.

Back inside, Bill Keeney slouched in his chair, a chair gifted to the town by a certain Jeremiah Bellows. That was way back then so many years ago - when Harry Mann's Garage was still in town, when the dump was still a dump and the riverfront wasn't much better. Jeremiah Bellows was Mayor back then, and, as Bill Keeney tells the story, it was Jeremiah Bellows who was first contacted about the gravestone. Mayor Bellows was descended on his mother's side from the town's founder, a man who reputedly burned a witch at the stake and suffered ever afterwards the indelible stain of her footprint on his tombstone. The latter day Bellows, however, was determined to make amends for that blot on his family legacy; he served his town with dignity and magnanimity towards all. He even offered "Honored Citizen" status to all descendants of the poor woman so victimized by his ancestor. When he finally passed on, he was so revered by certain members of the community that a plaque was placed at the entrance to the Town Offices, memorializing his pledge to those Honored Citizens of the town. And it was this plaque that was at issue in current Mayor Bill Keeney's encounter with the mysterious figure from the fog.

In the days that followed that meeting, the fog lifted, winter came and passed, and springtime came to the little town on the river. Property changed hands, folks divorced and remarried, and business thrived along Main Street. At the intersection with Hincks Street, busloads of tourists stopped at the Memorial Cemetery, where the town's founder, great ancestor of Bill Keeney, lay entombed under a ten-foot obelisk of granite. Newcomers gasped; cameras whirred and clicked. For there on the south facing facet of the stone was a shape, dark as an inkblot, the silhouette of a foot, the slender lower portion of a leg and a foot – a pointy foot, clearly a foot from one of those witches shrieking and dancing in etchings of yore. Nearby, a kiosk of sorts held brochures telling the history of the town, the story of the condemned woman, her curse upon the town's founder, and the efforts – unsuccessful – made over the

26

years to remove the stain from the tombstone. But always the stain came back. Tourists thrilled at the story; a larger parking lot was built at the cemetery to accommodate the buses; the town patted its coffers proudly and basked in its reputation as a tourist destination.

But this particular summer, the summer following the appearance of the figure from the fog in Mayor Keeney's office, something troubling began to happen. The foot on the obelisk began to fade, disappearing gradually like a slender figure dissolving into the fog. Tourists struggled with the settings on their cameras. Word spread and busloads of disgruntled travelers headed off to destinations elsewhere. Townsfolk could only watch in disbelief as their mark of distinction, such as it was, faded towards oblivion. The wellbeing of their town teetered in the balance.

Summer dissolved into fall, and wintertime approached. Again fog lay over the river when a soft knocking came at the office of Mayor Keeney. As before, a long pause in the hallway. And once again the slender figure confronting the Honorable Bill Keeney with piercing eyes. This time, the visitor was forceful and direct. She no longer wore her cowl, and her finger shook with rage.

"You've ignored our request." The voice was strong, emphatic, accusing.

"Our request? Mayor Keeney queried.

"Yes, *our* request."

Bill Keeney nodded warily.

"And you continue to refuse?"

"As I told you before, folks just don't notice." Bill Keeney's voice was shaky. A ghostly pallor had come over the face of his visitor.

"And your tourist attraction out there?" Her hand

waved in the general direction of *out there.* "That's good for business?"

Bill Keeney blinked his eyes and stared. Something was beginning to dawn on him. "Are you telling me..." he began. But he knew the answer to his own question.

His visitor nodded. "That's exactly what I'm telling you."

Bill Keeney felt a shiver run down his spine. "So this is a deal you're offering me?" he managed to say.

"Yes," his visitor said, "a deal, a pact, if you will."

"I put the silly plaque back up...."

"Not so silly plaque," the voice corrected.

"I see," said Bill Keeney. "And what do we get in return?"

"You get your silly tourist attraction, your stain on your stone, as it is."

"And that's it? The figure was growing fainter, more shadowy by the minute."

"No," came a voice from the distance. "There's one more thing."

Mayor Bill Keeney struggled to hear.

"Honored Citizen status in perpetuity for all descendants of the poor woman so victimized by your ancestor. As promised by your grandfather. As noted on the plaque."

The somewhat shaken Bill Keeney nodded and reached out his hand to seal the deal. But all he grasped was a handful of air.

"In perpetuity," came a voice from the fog outside.

In the days that followed, townsfolk rejoiced as the stain returned to the tombstone of their founder. And Bill Keeney kept his word: plaque returned to its place by the door and Honored Citizen status reaffirmed for all descendants of the woman condemned at the outset – many of whom remain among us to this day, their rights preserved – in perpetuity, as it may be.

A SALUTE
TO HARRY MANN'S GARAGE

It is morning at Harry Mann's Garage, and a harmless-looking, middle-aged gentleman has just entered the shop. His car waits outside, while he wanders about inside, attempting to make his presence known. He appears confused; he glances about nervously and pauses to get his bearings. To his right, just inside the overhead front door, a bulky mechanic circles an aging Pontiac, eyeing it critically. At the wheel of the car, an elderly woman dozes; apparently, she has been waiting for some time. Beyond, at mid-shop, a pair of feet extends from beneath a battered truck, and a grease-splattered figure sprawls over the fender of a Plymouth sedan, shiny rump up, like a shot-up cowboy slung over his saddle.

The customer – Walter Andrews, it says on a tag on his shirt - draws a deep breath, turns to his right, turns to his left, turns about and faces directly three old men in baggy pants and well-worn Eisenhower jackets, hunkered on a bench and observing him in silence. Their six eyes roll in sequence, as if fastened to a single crankshaft; they lean forward, and three quick, parallel shots of tobacco juice explode on the floor at their feet.

Walter Andrews turns away, spots at last a squat little knot of a man hunched on a seat under the cashier's window. "Arnie" it says on his shirt; he stares vacantly into the gloomy, overhead spaces. "Ahh..." sighs Walter Andrews. He approaches, clears his throat, announces that he has an eight o'clock appointment. Arnie continues to stare into the rafters. Walter prods him hesitantly. "Ít's, uh, for wheel-alignment." Arnie stretches and yawns but does not lower his gaze. "That's's, uh, wheel-alignment," repeats Walter. Arnie stirs. Laboriously, he hauls himself to his feet and pushes a button on a little two-way radio that hangs on the wall behind his seat. The back of his shirt reads: Harry Mann's Garage.

The radio crackles, spits out a voice. "I'm here, Arnie. Go ahead."

Arnie yawns into the speaker.

"Arnie?"

"Yuh, Harry. Yuh, there's a lady out front, the, uh, new minister's wife, Mrs. Sorenson. Says her lighter don't work. Sticks or something. You want us to take care of her this mornin'?"

"You got a man free? What's Bill doing?"

"Inspection. But he'll be done pretty soon."

"How 'bout Dick?"

"Brakes on the ambulance there."

"Smokey?"

"He ain't in yet."

"Hmmm... They need that ambulance in a hurry, Arnie?"

"Dunno, Harry."

"Well then, have Dick take care of Mrs. Sorenson."

"Okay, Harry. Whatever you say."

Arnie hangs up his phone and slumps back into his seat. The alignment customer stares at him in bewilderment, finally turns to the man called Bill, who now is tinkering with the blinkers on the old Pontiac, his back to Walter. The bench-sitters roll their eyes and watch impassively. At last, Bill stands up, leans across the dozing woman, and begins to scrape the expired sticker from her windshield. The woman awakes with a start, shrinks back into her seat.

31

"Turn to the right much?" Bill asks her, intent on his scraping.

"Nooo," mumbles the woman thoughtfully into his armpit, "not that I can think of."

"Good," says Bill. He pats the new sticker into place. "Just remember, if you ever *do* turn to the right, you wanna signal with your dimmer switch."

The woman smiles understandingly and promises to follow his instructions. Bill watches her intently, squinting a little. "Cross your heart?" he asks. The woman crosses her heart and backs from the garage.

By this time, there is a dazed look in the Walter's eyes. He turns back to Arnie, but Arnie has disappeared down a rut in the floor, past benches piled high with nuts, bolts, water pumps, grinding wheels, lathes, alternators, and great chunks of rusted iron, into the gloom at the back of the shop. He reappears now, limping and shuffling down his rut, stopping to adjust the angle of the feet under the old Dodge, stopping again at a Coke machine, and returning, finally, to his two-way radio, sucking at a bottle of Coca-Cola. He pokes at the radio, and Harry's voice comes through again. "I'm here, Arnie. What is it?"

Arnie studies his reflection in the cashier's window.

"Arnie?"

Arnie puts down his Coke. "Yuh, Harry. I got Dick on Mrs. Sorenson's lighter."

"Okay, Arnie. How's that ambulance coming?"

"Dunno, Harry. I'll get Dick back on it soon's he's done with Mrs. Sorenson."

"Sounds good, Arnie."

"Okay, Harry. Whatever you say."

Arnie slumps back into his seat, the Coke clutched in

his lap and his eyes rolled upwards. Walter Andrews stares at him uncomprehendingly; his hands have begun to shake slightly. He turns to Bill again for help, but Bill has moved to the back of the shop, where he putters about, oiling and polishing the alignment machine. Nearby, a shiny ambulance, minus its front wheels, squats on its haunches, brake parts strewn about on the floor. A glimmer of hope comes to Walter's eyes, and he walks quickly to the back of the garage.

"Hello, there," warbles Bill. "You the one with the shimmy in the front end?"

Walter stands dumbstruck, finally manages to stammer something about his eight o'clock appointment.

"Well then, drive 'er right in," pipes Bill.

Walter bobs his head, squares his shoulders, and marches off, past the critical gazes of the bench-sitters and out of the shop. Shortly, he appears at the back door, driving a late-model Ford. Bill guides him on to the alignment machine and begins to circle the car, humming to himself and altogether ignoring Walter, who now hovers in the background like a nervous, expectant father.

At this point, a lanky, stoop-shouldered young man drifts through the back door and curls past the alignment machine. "'Bout time you got here, Smokey," calls out Bill, scratching his head and gazing at nothing in particular. Smokey ignores him and weaves his way to the front of the shop, swatting, in passing, the rump slung over the Plymouth fender. A dull wooden thud echoes through the garage. With the fading of the echo, Smokey returns, rolling beside him a pair of well-worn tires. Close on his heels, comes a stout little bulldog of a man. They stop and palaver across a tire-changing machine that mushrooms from a pool of oil at the back of the shop.

"Now, were them blackwalls or whitewalls you wanted?" Smokey asks, goggling and scratching his armpit.

"Cost the same?" The man eyes Smokey suspiciously.

"Nope."

"What's the difference?"

"Two bucks."

"Gimme blackwalls, then," says the man. "I'll be back in an hour. That okay with you?"

"Fine with me," says Smokey. "Jeez, I gotta..." he adds, clutching the seat of his pants and heading for the men's room. The fat little man consults his watch and waddles from the shop.

Back at the alignment machine, Bill is sitting on a creeper, half under the front of the Ford, arranging his tools and preparing his assault. Behind him, Walter Andrews has begun to pace back and forth; he stoops suddenly now at the blast of a horn from the front of the shop.

Bill hears the blast too. "Oopsie," he says, lumbering to his feet. He winks at Walter. "Inspection," he explains and ambles off. Walter stares after him, head hung forward, mouth slightly agape. He retreats to his post in the shadow of the alignment machine.

Half an hour passes. Smokey emerges from the men's room, grinning to himself and buckling his belt. He whistles a few bars but stops when he sees the tires. A look of befuddlement crosses his face, but he soon gathers his wits and wanders off, returning shortly with a pair of flashy-looking whitewall tires. These he deposits near the tire-changing machine before wandering off again for a cup of coffee.

Throughout, Walter has been regarding Smokey with a look of something bordering on astonishment. Bill has not yet returned from his inspection, and now, with Smokey slouched against the wall, sipping coffee and staring balefully at the tires, Walter is moved to action. He approaches Smokey. By this point, an element of determination might be detected in his step, an element, perhaps, of desperation. "Those tires, there," he says to Smokey, pointing with a quivering finger, those are whitewalls, aren't they?"

Smokey blinks his eyes and shakes himself from his trance. "Huh?" he says.

Walter repeats his question.

"Them there?" says Smokey, pointing at the tires and grinning proudly. "Sure them're whitewalls."

"But I'm sure I heard the man say he wanted blackwalls."

Smokey tucks his head between his shoulders and leers at Walter. "Lookee here," he says at last. He balances one of the tires on edge, supporting the top with the index finger of his left hand. With his right hand, he points to the white wall of the tire. "Whitewall," he says in the voice of a three-year-old instructing a two-year-old. He flicks his finger, spinning the tire 180 degrees, and points to the back of the tire. "Blackwall," he intones in the same childlike voice. Then he repeats the lesson, only faster this time. Again and again, he repeats the lesson, faster and faster, until the tire is a spinning blur, and he is whooping, over and over again in rapid-fire succession, "Whitewall, blackwall, whitewall, blackwall...":

Walter shrinks back, clutching his head. He is visibly shaken. With a shadow of something like fear on his face, he watches from his post at the alignment machine as Smokey winds down, kicks the discarded tires a few times, and slouches against the wall for a cigarette.

At this point, Bill returns, winks again at Walter, and lowers himself onto his creeper. Meticulously, like a manicurist, he picks through his tools, selects a wrench, and disappears beneath the Ford. Shortly, he emerges, summoned by loud honking from the front of the shop. He shrugs apologetically. "'Nother inspection," he mumbles, ambling off. When he returns, some twenty minutes later, Walter has not moved; he stands frozen in the shadows, fingers twitching almost imperceptibly. Bill glances at him, shrugs, and returns to his business under the Ford.

Minutes pass. Then, with a creaking of creeper wheels, Bill emerges again. Clucking and chirping to himself, he selects a baby sledge hammer from his toolbox and rolls himself back under the Ford. Gentle tapping noises ensue, gradually grow more vehement, mingle with grunts from Bill and shrieks from the wheels of the creeper. And then comes silence, followed by a heavy sigh from Bill, by more squealing and grunting, by ponderous shiftings of human bulk. Another silence, a sinister, ill-boding hush, culminating at last in a thunderous, reverberating crash. The Ford shudders; its trunk springs open; a thin crack darts across its windshield, and a rusted, grease-covered balljoint pops out, rolls and shimmies across the floor, and comes to rest, at last, between the feet of Walter Andrews. Bill follows on his creeper, sits gazing at the dislodged balljoint, shaking his head and daintily wiping his hands on a rag. "Well, now," he chirps at last, "we got the little bugger, didn't we?"

Walter stares at him, eyes wide, mouth twisting and

contorting, struggling to speak.

"New one should be in first of the week," Bill adds, laboring to his feet and returning to his tools.

Veins bulge and throb in Walter's neck. A violent shudder runs across his shoulders. He points a furiously shaking finger at Bill, sweeps his arm across the shop in a gesture of utter disbelief, staggers backwards, and slumps against the fender of the ambulance.

Bill observes impassively, clucking a little to himself, then bobs his head and begins to wipe off his tools. He stands, polishing a large crescent wrench, watching, as the customer gasps, struggles for breath, and, falls to the floor.

At the front of the shop, Arnie, apparently sensing a familiar tremor, hoists himself to his feet and shuffles down his rut. Approaching the front-end machine, he jerks his head towards the fallen customer and glares inquiringly at Bill. Bill shrugs and glances away towards the tire-changing machine, where Smokey is slouched against the wall, watching and grinning idiotically. Suddenly, he stoops, picks up a tire, and begins spinning it. "Whitewall," he giggles. "Whitewall, blackwall, whitewall, blackwall..."

Bill bobs his head and grins at Arnie. Arnie rolls his eyes and returns to the front of the shop. There, he slumps back into his seat and, for long minutes, contemplates the darkness beyond the rafters, before laboring to his feet again and activating his two-way radio.

"Uh... Harry?"

"Yuh, Arnie, I'm here. What is it?"

"That alignment customer, Harry?"

"Huh?"

"Man in for alignment, Harry?"

"Yuh, Arnie. What about him?"

"He's sorta lyin' on the floor, Harry. Don't look so good."

"He movin'at all?"

"Dunno, Harry. I can get Dick to check – soon's he's done with Mrs. Sorenson there."

"You do that, Arnie."

"Sure thing, Harry."

"Uh, Arnie?"

"Yuh, Harry?"

"Lyin' on the floor, you said, Arnie?"

"That's what I said, Harry."

"Uh, look, Arnie... I better call a ambulance. Get right back to you."

"Sure thing, Harry... I'll be right here."

Arnie drops back into his seat and gazes to the back of the shop, where Bill is polishing his tools and Smokey is gleefully bouncing an over-inflated tire. He shifts his gaze to the front, past the bench-sitters and through the window to where Dick's feet protrude from the driver's window of Mrs. Sorenson's late-model sedan. He looks away, rolls his eyes upwards, slumps deeper in his seat. At last, his radio buzzer sounds. Arnie yawns and struggles to his feet.

"Yuh, Harry, what is it?"

"Uh, Arnie, how's Dick comin' on that ambulance there?"

"Dunno, Harry. He's still workin' on Mrs. Sorenson's lighter. They need it in a hurry?"

"Depends, Arnie. Is that guy still lyin' on the floor?"

"Near's I can tell from here, Harry."

"Uh, look, Arnie, you better get Dick back on that ambulance."

"Right now, Harry?"

"Soon's he's finished with Mrs. Sorenson."

"Okay, Harry, whatever you say." Arnie hangs up his phone and settles back into his seat.

Meanwhile, at the back of the shop, Smokey has approached the stricken customer and now stands over him, a look of imbecilic glee on his face. He pokes the customer with his toe; there is no response. He pokes harder; still no response. He cocks his foot and kicks the customer sharply on the funny bone. Nothing. Satisfied, Smokey rolls the body onto Bill's creeper, grips it by the ankles, and pushes it, wheelbarrow-style, across the shop. At the old Plymouth, he stops, adjusts his grip, and pushes the body underneath, until only the feet protrude. He returns to his tire-changing machine.

Bill looks up from his tool-polishing. "You'll be wantin' to get some anti-freeze into that pretty quick," he calls to Smokey.

"Betcher ass," Smokey calls back. He struggles to balance a tire on his fingertip, fails. "Soon's I finish with these tires."

At the front of the shop now, Arnie is slumped deep in his seat, snoring loudly. The bench-sitters are grunting and chewing and spitting in three-part harmony, while the round little bulldog of a man stands just inside the front door, adjusting his eyes to the darkness and glancing about uncertainly.

THE DEERSLAYERS

Deep in the evergreen forest, at the edge of a large, swampy tract, a great, branchy pine grows tall and proud among its underlings. Wolf pine, it is called by some. Deep in the evergreen forest – deer country, it is called. An old tote road passes through, passes through the shadow of the great, whispering pine.

Deer hunting season approaches. Great, antlered bucks glide through the swamp, glide through the dreams of eager hunters, halt in the cross-hairs of cold, blue eyes.

And the day before opening: Jack Beene and Muletrain O'Brien pad down the tote road, pass through the silence of the evergreen forest.

"Lotsa sign," says Jack. That's what his grandfather used to say about deer tracks in the cedar break and antler rubbings on the tree trunks. Venison to be had. Jack loves this forest, the shadows and the solitude.

"Unnh," answers Muletrain. Lotsa sign: deer track, coon track, boot track, Jeep track, spent birdshot shells, stump top ashtrays, Schlitz cans glimmering here and there – others have passed before.

They approach the swamp. Jack stops in his tracks.

"Hey, Muletrain...."

"Unnh?"

"Good stand over there. Up the big pine."

Muletrain appraises the tree. "Unnh," he says. They grope their way down a rabbit run through the underbrush and stand at the base of the great tree, gazing up into its branches.

"Good stand," says Jack.

"Unnh," says Muletrain.

"Get there before daylight," says Jack.

They retrace the rabbit run to the road and pad again through the forest. "Lotsa sign," says Jack. "Lotsa... Afternoon, Sam; didn't see you coming; out a little early, aintcha, heh, heh, heh. Lotsa sign," he mutters to himself, "lotsa sign. Good stand, too, good stand. Afternoon, Pete; out a little early, aintcha, heh, heh, heh. That Mark comin along behind you? Yep, it's Mark, all right. Afternoon, Mark..." And so they pass from the forest.

It is dark, very dark, in the small hours before opening sunrise. Jack leads the way by faltering flashlight. "Watch your step there, Muletrain," he says in a loud whisper. "Over the log there... Okay, here we are. Just get through these – ouch, goddammit – briars. Okay, here we are. You there, Muletrain? I can see it now. Yep, right on the old button."

They stand at the base of the tree. The flashlight dims to a faint glow. "Oh, Christ," curses Jack. He shakes the light; it goes out altogether. "Dammitall!" he says. "Now what are we gonna do?" He heaves the flashlight into the darkness; there is a distant, soggy thud. Jack draws a deep breath. "Okay, Muletrain," he exhales, "we gotta climb the tree in the dark. You all set?"

Heaving and grunting in the great pine now. Groping and weaving of guns and bodies through ragged branches. A dull thud – boot on flesh. "Jeezum Christ Almighty! My nose is smashed all t'hell!"

"Sorry about that, Muletrain. Real sorry. Hold on; we're gettin' up there now. .."

Rustling in the branches, bumping of bodies. "Sorry about that, Muletrain. Didn't know you was there. Hold on now; we're almost there. Oh Jeezum, was that your hand

Muletrain? Sorry, real sorry about that."

More rustlings and gropings. "We're up there good now, Muletrain," says Jack. All's we gotta do now is sit and wait. Find a good branch and make ourselves comfy."

Minutes pass. "You comfy over there, Muletrain? Not much longer now, not much longer..."

Darkness persists. Faint groaning and rustlings from the great tree. And slowly, the blackness begins to lift. The tree silhouettes black on gray-black. Faint light spreads through the forest, a cold glow on the swamp, drawing eager eyes fixed, transfixed, to the spaces below.

More light, and more. And then suddenly, brightness... And there, there on the far edge of the swamp, standing with one foot lifted, expectant, delicately sniffing the dawn, the vision incarnate, the buck primogenitor, the granddaddy, they say, of all bucks.

The great tree quivers, then steadies, stiffens, and holds for an instant stock-still.

A thunderous roar shatters the dawn. Needles, twigs, branches fall from the great tree; spent cartridges pelt like hail on the ground below. A great cry fills the swamp, as hunters, two, three, ten, dozens, scores perhaps, scamper like squirrels through the branches, scurry down the great trunk, and race madly into the dawn.

Muletrain, who had fallen asleep at the base of the tree when the flashlight went out and was awakened by the daybreak fusillade, is the first to reach the riddled carcass and lay claim to the venison. Close on his heels comes Jack. "Jeezum," puffs Jack. "Jeezum Criminy." He eyes the carcass. "Ain't so big as he looked now, is he, Muletrain? Ain't so big at all." He shakes his head. "Eighty, ninety pounds, maybe. Not so much to brag about." He turns to face the crowd behind him. "Eighty, maybe ninety pounds," he repeats. "Lotsa lead, though," he muses. "Nother ten, maybe twenty pounds." He continues to shake his head.

While across the swamp, the great branchy pine, empty at last, stands tall and proud among its underlings. Deep in the evergreen forest.

SNIPERS WERE EVERYWHERE

Folks were scared back then. Doomsday seemed imminent. Books were written, bunkers were built, and survivalist groups flourished. My own book was titled, simply enough, *Survive!* I read it fourteen times, blueprinting my subconscious and tuning my instincts accordingly. And just in the nick of time, too.

The following day, I found myself floundering in what my book called a sea of humanity, a vast horde of panicking individuals. I felt the telltale pressure on my elbows, felt myself about to be crushed, drawn down by the undertow. Instinctively, I bunched up my arms and lifted my feet off the ground. And there I was. just as the book had promised, bobbing like a duck in a millpond.

There was only one problem. This was America, and everyone was concerned with survival. The entire crowd had read the book or heard of it on talk shows. They all hunched up their arms, too, and lifted up their feet, until we sat there like so many frogs on a lily pad. A monk walked by then, with flowing robes and a book of numbers. He looked at us, and all he said was, "Beautiful." According to my book, he should have made himself as inconspicuous as possible and walked, not run, quickly away from the crowd.

That night, I lay awake for many hours, contemplating the monk's behavior, the situation in general, reviewing my survivalist readings and the precautions I had taken. My thoughts were rudely interrupted, however, and bore no fruit. Chaos erupted, total dislocation and breakdown of all systems. Fortunately, I had made all necessary precautions. In my bunker, there was no time for thought, time only for hoarding my three-week supply of food, shooting marauders, explaining to friends and neighbors less prepared than myself that this was survival we were talking about, not brotherhood, before shooting them also. (These explanations, incidentally, were in violation of the book's instructions. "Don't talk," the book said. "Shoot for the head or chest.") Fortunately, my ammunition held out.

Unfortunately, my situation went downhill from there. Three weeks later, food gone, I found myself on my own, beyond the scope of my readings. Two things I knew for sure. One, I was starving and needed help. Two, anyone still alive was a survivalist. I knew something about survivalists. I chose slow starvation, foraging, gnawing on roots in the shadows of my bunker.

It was then that the monk returned. His robes were singed and torn. In place of his book, he carried granola. How had he managed to survive? I asked. He tapped his chest. "Kevlar," he said, "bulletproof." His head? Kevlar, too. He lifted his mask, a bulletproof visor, revealing a face remarkably similar to my own. I shrugged and ate granola. (This response to the monk, incidentally, was sheer thoughtlessness, a flagrant violation of the book's code; I should have shot him in the head when he lifted his visor.)

That night, I made up for my mistakes. I pumped my remaining ammunition into the eyehole of the mask. To my surprise, the monk was not there, having stepped outside the bunker to urinate. He stood in the doorway now, while I stood naked, caught in the act and without ammunition. Hand-to-hand combat, I thought, death blows, a chop to the thorax. At the last moment, however, Chapter Eight flashed in my mind, a cautionary footnote: "Be reasonable: retreat in the face of superior force."

I chose the course of reason. The monk, so like myself in every facet and dimension, had about him an aura of extraordinary quickness and strength. In the morning, I followed him from the bunker; he had the granola, after all. I followed him, cringing in his shadow; snipers were everywhere, and he wore the armor.

FROM HERE TO YUCCA FLAT: HOMAGE TO HOMEBREW

Hunkered in the broccoli I am, weeding, basking in the good things of life, when my silence is shattered violently by the thunderous clatter of hoofbeats. Never in my little world of nanny goats and homebrew and organic cabbage have I heard such a sound. Full of fury and vengeance it is, iron-shod hooves pounding the roadway. Shivering with terror, I crouch in the cornstalks. Below, the roadway is empty, but the clatter of hoofbeats grows louder, louder, as rounding the corner they come, thirty-five degrees off vertical, two towering figures on wild, snorting steeds. Cutting they come, crouching and springing up the driveway, gravel pelting like hail on the pavement below.

"Hyah!" Foam flecks flying, feet rearing and prancing, black hides glistening, and riders viciously reining. "Whoa, theah, Satan!" "Whoa, theah, Sheba!" They come to a halt in the chard.

Horses pawing. Eyes squinting. "Who that over there, Clint?" The woman: black-clad with silver spangles. Tall, lean, tough – long shadow penetrating the cornstalks like a finger accusing.

Clint's voice, high and raspy. "Don't rightly know, Babe." More squinting. "Hey, you! You there, skulkin' around in the cornstalks. Come on out here, Sonny. Let's have a look at you."

Behind me, only the summer squashes – no escape there. I emerge from the corn patch and stand among the radishes, wiggling my toes in the warm soil, eyeing the jackhammer hooves of the two wild stallions.

"Har, har, looky there, Clint. He don't even have no

47

shoes on."

"Hey, Sonny," calls the man.

I dig my toes in deeper, draw strength and courage from the rich, earthy soil, the smell of arugula nearby. "Welcome to Daffodil Acres," I manage to say. "What can I do for you?"

The desperado hoots. "Hear that, Babe? Daffodil Acres!" Howling and knee-slapping. Loosening of reins. The stallions drop their heads and grab mouthfuls of chard.

"Hey you, Satan! Hey you, Sheba. Git away from that stuff. Rabbit food. Shrivel your balls."

Heads yanked up – but already a softening in the eyes of the stallions. They nicker softly, and I offer them carrots, one in each hand. Whips whistle, lashing my wrists. But too late – the horses have eaten the carrots. I shake my hands free, step back, freeze in the cross-glares from Clint and Babe.

"Try that again, Sonny," hisses Babe, "and I'll shoot your balls from here to Yucca Flat." She draws a shiny six-gun and aims at my crotch. Instinctively, I cover with my hands.

Clint roars. "Har-de-har-har, now don't he look like a little lady, all barefoot and bashful." He leans forward in his saddle. "Now you listen to me, Sonny. We're two hungry and thirsty hombres, and it don't seem to me like you're showin' us much hospitality. Now you throw me one of them there tomatoes, Sonny." He motions to the tomato patch with the barrel of his six-gun.

I steady my hands, then select the ripest tomato of the lot and toss it to Clint. Six shots ring out in rapid succession. Tomato pulp plasters the pea vines. "What I mean to say, Sonny," Clint sneers, "is rabbit food ain't hospitality." Cooly, he blows smoke from the barrel of his revolver.

"B-b-but," I stammer, "that was an all-organic Burpee beefsteak tomato."

Clint's eyes light up. "Beefsteak," he muses thoughtfully. He slips from his saddle and stands tall in the parsley. Babe slips down beside him, fully half a head taller. Clint's fingers dig into my shoulder. "Let's you and me go on up to the house there, Sonny, and talk about beefsteak."

I hesitate, watching the stallions demolish the chard. Babe taps the base of my skull with the barrel of her six-gun. "Beefsteak," she says. "Remember?" Behind her, the stallions head for the goat pasture, nickering and calling softly. I lead the way to the house, Babe right behind me, the barrel of her six-gun lodged in the small of my back.

Inside, Clint slaps his gun on the table, covers it with his hat, tips back in his chair, feet on the table, gouging the Minwax polyurethane finish with the points of his spurs. Across from him, Babe leans, elbows on the table. She toys with her revolver, stroking its barrel. She removes her hat, shaking long, raven tresses loose over her shoulders. She is stunningly beautiful. I catch my breath, pretend to cough, glance out the window, see the stallions nuzzling the goats through the pasture fence.

With a thundering crash, Clint sinks a spur into the tabletop. "Beefsteak!" he roars. I shudder, cast through my mind – lentils, tofu, the veggie casserole simmering in the oven?

Babe saves the moment. "Whiskey," she drawls. "First whiskey, then beefsteak." She is grinning now, lounging in her chair, full, spangled breasts straining at satin like ripening eggplant.

Clint sinks his second spur into the antique oak. "Whiskey!" he thunders. "First whiskey, then beefsteak."

"I-I'm sorry," I stammer, "but I do have herb tea..."

"Shee-yit!" Clint struggles to his feet.

"Herb tea!" mocks Babe. She eyes me down the barrel of her six-gun. "Where?"

I point to a box on the windowsill. *Kapow!* Glass shatters, mellow mint rises, falls, settles like volcanic ash. "Whiskey!" hisses Babe.

I glance out the window. The stallions have jumped the fence and are gamboling with the goats. My spirits lift. "I d-do have some homebrew," I offer.

"Homebrew!" Clint explodes. "By god, homebrew. I haven't had homebrew since I was knee-high to a rattlesnake. Sonny, bring on the homebrew."

I steady my hands, remove a growler of homebrew from the refrigerator, manage to pour it off into a pitcher without the telltale cloud of sediment. The mere sight of the clear, bubbling liquid gives me courage. "Homebrew," I declare proudly, setting the pitcher on the table and fetching two thick mugs.

Clint squints at me through one eye. "Nother glass," he says, his voice commanding. "You gonna drink with us."

I comply, fill the three mugs to the frothy limit. "Prosit," I offer.

"Drink, you asshole," says Clint. He blows his froth on the table. Babe follows suit. They watch me sip delicately, then drain their glasses.

Clint belches, pounds his empty mug on the table. "Couple of *thirsty* hombres," he drawls to no one in particular. I refill their glasses, sit back, sipping and watching.

Babe catches my eye. "Drink," she orders. I drink, and Babe refills my glass. I drink that, too. I am not worried; this is *my* homebrew; I know how to handle it. I feel my courage rising.

Clint slides his mug across the table to Babe. "Fill 'er up, doll," he grunts.

Babe slides the mug back. "Fill 'er up yourself, Clinty," she says sweetly sharp.

Clint jerks his feet off the table, then shrugs at me and refills his mug. "Don't s'pose it much matters who pours the stuff," he mumbles. I detect a slight slurring of his speech; I watch Clint rub the gouges in the table with his thumb.

"Oh, looky," cries Babe, draining her glass and pointing out the window. "The horsies are playing with the goaties."

Clint glances out the window. "Good for 'em," he mumbles. "new friends never hurt no one." He turns to me; he even looks different now; bean sprouts and homebrew have been known to work wonders. "Nice place you got here, Sonny," Clint says. He continues to rub the gouges in the table with his thumb. "Got some putty, I'll patch this up for you."

Babe eyes him shrewdly, then smiles knowingly at me. "Relax," she whispers. "He's just a big pussycat."

I smile and wink at her. "Okay," I say. "Casserole's in the oven. You get that. I'll get the putty."

Babe moves gracefully, if a little drunkenly, to the oven and fits an apron over her holsters. I place a can of putty in front of Clint and watch as he works it into the gouges with the butt of his six-gun. Babe dishes out the casserole – bean sprouts, lentils, brown rice, and tofu. They eat hungrily.

"Mmmmm," says Babe.

"Good enough for ten hungry hombres," says Clint. He wolfs down his third helping, washes it down with a mug of homebrew. I stand up, clap him on the shoulder. "Well, Clint, old boy," I say cheerily, "time to get to work. After the dishes, there's some patching up needs doing down in the garden."

Clint grins up at me agreeably. "Sure thing, boss. Nothin' like some good old-fashioned work t'make a man feel good." He moves to the sink and rolls up his sleeves. I collect the six-guns and drop them down the compost chute, then sit at the table, close and catty-corner to Babe. She has removed her neckerchief and holsters. Behind us, the splashing of dishwater and clinking of plates; here, Babe so close and inviting. I stroke her hand and gaze deep into her eyes.

"Dishes all done, boss," Clint sings out behind us.

"Wash out the sink?" I ask without looking around.

Splashing of water. "All done, boss. What next?"

I wink at Babe, slide away from the table. Clint is drying his hands on a dishtowel. "Follow me," I say. I lead Clint down to the garden, explain the work that needs doing – several hours worth of patching, replanting, and weeding. "You're a good boy, Clint," I say. Clint smiles at me gratefully.

Back at the house, Babe is reclining on the sofa. I stand, gazing down at her, relishing my prospects. "You'll want to take those boots off," I say softly. "Be right back."

"Clint," I call from the window. "When you're done with the garden, I want you to hitch up those horses and plow up the north pasture."

"Sure thing, boss," Clint calls back. "Be done by nightfall."

I return to the sofa. Babe is struggling with her boots. She looks ravishing. 'Here," I offer, "let me help you with your socks..."

And so it goes, day after lovely day – tofu, bean sprouts, fresh organic produce from the garden, dawn until dusk, Clint laboring in the garden, splitting cord upon cord of winter firewood, growing stronger and healthier by the hour; myself, day after day, sipping my homebrew and languishing with Babe. And Babe, oh, yes, Babe – finding more and more pleasure in the simple homesteading virtues, as she draws yet another loaf of fresh-baked bread from the oven, brews mellow mint tea from the remnants swept up from the windowsill.

Until, one morning, IT happens – Babe gazing at Clint in a warm, most appreciative manner. I've been waiting for this. I watch them closely, then slip away to the barn.

Satan was always my favorite. Through his weeks of languishing, several things there were that I did not neglect. One was Satan's diet. Nothing organic or homegrown there. Straight urea-laden, Purina feed it was, 20% pure protein. Now, the stallion paws at his stall. His coat glistens, his eye is wild. I cinch the saddle tight, ram the bit into his mouth. From a grain bag, I pull Clint's hombre outfit, meticulously altered during Babe's afternoon naps, complete with spangles, holsters, and six-guns rescued from the compost chute. Now, I don the outfit and mount the stallion. Brandishing the six-guns, I sail over the pasture fence. With scattering gravel and thundering hoofbeats, rounding the corner I go, thirty-five degrees off vertical. Due west! Iron-shod hooves pounding the pavement. "To arms, to arms," I cry, "the zucchinis are ripening!"

Behind me, the sounds of Clint's ax ring through the air – and the softer sounds of Babe, calling the goats for their morning milking.

IN SIGNIFICANT ACTION

(Author's Note: Do not read this story if you frustrate easily. The narrator is unreliable, and the protagonist, Charlie, is unstable at best. Charlie has left his safe haven, a community of like-minded friends, in rural Maine and is now wandering around the City of Bangor, in the aftermath of some act of political sabotage he seems to have executed the night before.)

Charlie stood at the corner of Broadway and 17th Street, his back to a utility pole and his hands limp by his sides. His head was tilted back, exposing the stubble on his jaw to the first rays of the morning sun. Charlie was breathing hard. To a close observer, his eyes might have reflected an odd blend of fear and excitement – mostly fear. But there were no close observers. It was 5:30AM, and Charlie was alone on the street, conspicuously alone.

As Charlie's breath returned, as he felt the warmness of the sun on his face and saw the new day dawning, saw, too, that he was alone on the street, his fear dwindled to the point where he shrugged it off altogether. No one had followed him after all. And now, the scene of the—well, of the action – was half a state behind him. Perhaps hitchhiking hadn't been the best getaway plan; certainly, blurting out his story, complete with details and political rationale, to the yawning driver of the truck that had picked him up had not been very professional. But then again, here he was, safe and undetected. His long run from the turnpike exit hadn't even been necessary. The driver had probably thought he was making the whole thing up. No matter: it would be common knowledge soon enough.

Meanwhile, there was this aroma of bacon to be dealt with.

Charlie sniffed the air and scanned his surroundings. From half a block away, he pinpointed the source of the aroma – a vent on Joe's Café, broadcasting the breakfast menu. Charlie's head, not a proven leader in its own right, now took orders from his stomach.

"Two eggs," he told Joe, "bacon, toast – make that three eggs, over easy. Have you heard the news?"

Charlie was suddenly aware of not being alone in the diner. Forks froze in mid-air, spoons in mid-stir. Chewing ground to a halt; heads swiveled. From across the counter, belly and biceps ballooning his T-shirt to its greasy limits, Joe glared at him.

"Whazzat?" Joe grunted.

"Why, uh, uh, I thought something happened last night, something..."

The silence thickened around him; his words skittered like grease on a hot griddle. Charlie squirmed. "I mean, I mean, the Red Sox won, didn't they? I thought the Red Sox won last night."

Joe wiped his mouth with the back of his hand and turned away. "Got their asses beat," growled a voice from a booth behind Charlie. Other voices from other booths: "...asshole ... hippie ...shithead..."

Charlie backed off, ignored the "Sheesh!" of contempt, and sipped his coffee. He was sure of one thing at least: he had outstripped the news. Oh well, it would arrive soon enough. Meanwhile, he'd better be a little more careful, eat his breakfast, get cleaned up, find Molly's apartment...

YES, find Molly's apartment! She'd said he could stay there, hide out for a few days. Of course, she'd thought he was joking about the whole thing, but never mind that...

Charlie's breakfast shot across the counter and skidded to a stop at his elbow. Charlie did not look up; looking down was sufficient: one shriveled piece of bacon, no butter for the toast, egg yokes marbled with the whites and cooked to the consistency of cheese. But Charlie did not complain. Hungrily, he ate his breakfast, paid Joe, and made his exit. Behind him, the voices: "Feller looks nervous ... shithead ... junkie..." Charlie knew he had made their day.

Outside, it was still early morning, but traffic had picked up considerably. Good, he was part of the crowd now – though he was probably the only one running on adrenalin rather than sleep. He stood on the stoop of Joe's Café and surveyed his position. Two blocks away, a phone booth seemed to hover slightly above the pavement in the flat morning light. Charlie sauntered towards it. The night's activity, the food in his stomach, the promise of a new day – Charlie's spirits were beginning to lift. On an impulse, he slipped into the phone booth and dialed the police.

"Yeah, hello..." His words sounded like pebbles rattling inside a glass jar. The voice at the other end sounded like a gravel crusher. Charlie pressed on. "That business last night? Have you caught whoever did it yet?" At his ear, the sound of a distant rockslide. Grinding and grating. "Listen, my name's not Buster. It's.... never mind." And Charlie hung up.

So, he was still ahead of the news. No matter, it would be on the air soon enough. In the newspapers, too. And *pictures*. Charlie rubbed his hands together. No hurry.

Then again, it did seem odd, the police not knowing. He would have expected an alert, an all-points-bulletin, something like that. He pulled a crumpled piece of paper from his pocket and flattened it on the shelf under the telephone. Most of the paper was covered with a crude map, marked with red X's. In the lower right hand corner, it said: Molly Adamson, 569-4771. It was still too early to call, but Charlie flipped through the phone book, looking for an address: Adams, Adamson: Claude, Hiram, Xavier. But no Molly. Still, no matter; he had her number; he'd call her later. She'd *said* he could stay there. Of course, she'd been smiling, humoring him a little, never thinking he would actually...

Siren screaming, a police car shot by Charlie's booth and screeched to a halt. More sirens. Charlie hid his face in the phone book, felt his muscles tense, tighten to the point of... Bolting from the phone booth, Charlie cut to his left and darted down an alley. Behind him, a police radio blared. Charlie ran, ran as he had already run once that morning, ran until the realization suddenly struck him that, once again, no one was following him. This was getting absurd.

Panting heavily, Charlie slowed to a walk. He was in a little park now, trees and grass and flowers surrounded by pavement and traffic. He chose a bench hidden from the path by shrubbery and sat down among the pigeon droppings. Ahead of him, in the roots of the shrubbery, a landscape of litter: shreds of newspaper, styrofoam cups, condoms, pop-tops glittering here and there. "Pigs!" spat Charlie. And with that, a manifesto he had once written flashed through his mind: Greed. Waste. Throwaway culture. Corporate tyranny. Military industrial. More greed. Charlie couldn't take it all at that hour of the morning. He looked away, gazing up into the treetops. He closed his eyes. Soon he was dozing.

"Been here all night, Buster?" The voice grated. Charlie blinked his eyes. A young patrolman, #836 by his badge, stood over him, tapping his nightstick in the palm of his hand.

Charlie jolted to his senses. "Uh, no, no," he said."I wasn't even..." But he caught himself in time. "What I mean to say is..."

The policeman pointed his nightstick at Charlie, then at a park sign: "Park Closed 8PM – 7AM." In the distance, a clock chimed. Charlie held up eight fingers, grinning. The policeman grinned back, nodding his head and thwacking his palm with his nightstick. Then he winked maliciously and ambled off.

Whew! Charlie was of two minds. In one, he was the performing artist, eagerly awaiting the next morning's reviews. In the other, he was acutely and increasingly aware that the performance in question was well beyond the limits of the law and bore penalties of the severest nature. In either case, he'd better move around a little, reconnoiter, try to get in touch with Molly. He could use his bench as a base of operations.

When Charlie returned to his bench an hour or so later, he was clutching a large cup of steaming coffee and cradling four hotdogs in a morning newspaper. With the real estate page, he wiped a three-foot section clean of pigeon droppings and set himself up for the morning. Molly hadn't answered her phone; he must have missed her, shouldn't have waited so long. No matter; he'd catch her later. Besides, he's found something else, just a few blocks away, a downtown Sears outlet with a quarter-acre TV display in the window. Twelve different brands to choose from, tuned simultaneously to twenty-three different channels. Gawd! Molly could wait. The evening news would be mind-boggling – reporters everywhere, film footage, analysis, interpretations of the significance.... But, shit, what if they missed the point? No way. Munching his hotdogs, Charlie banished the thought and turned his attention to the newspaper in his lap. A gust of wind deposited his hotdog wrappers among the litter in the shrubbery, but Charlie did not notice.

Sipping his coffee now, Charlie scanned his newspaper. By this point, his expectations had waned considerably. It would be nice if there were a little something in the newspaper, but the electronic media was where it was at, the evening news. Only a cartoon caught his attention: a child standing with a nuclear power plant in the background and a foot growing from his head. And a passerby saying, "Why Henry, you've grown a foot since I last saw you."

Charlie chuckled to himself as his Styrofoam cup skittered away into the shrubbery. He did not retrieve it. For a moment, he thought he saw Patrolman #836 lurking behind the bushes. "No way," he murmured to himself. "Figment of my imagination." He folded his newspaper and closed his eyes. Soon he was fast asleep, a sitting duck for the pigeons overhead. Charlie didn't notice.

"Hey, Buddy! Hey, you wantcher crossword puzzle?"

Charlie jerked to full alert. His heart was pounding. Jesus, he'd grown complacent. Five minutes? Five hours? How long had he been sleeping? And who...? Wakefulness percolated through Charlie's system. Nervously, he glanced about, saw only a grizzled, unwashed figure six feet down the bench, eyeing him shrewdly.

"Your crossword puzzle," his benchmate repeated.

"You want it?"

Charlie inhaled deeply. Relax, he told himself. Just a bum, a wino no doubt. He passed his newspaper to the man. "Heard the news?" he asked casually. The man grinned at him and shrugged his shoulders. Charlie returned to his dozing.

"Criminal?" The voice was hoarse and harsh. "Six down. Criminal. Ten letters"

Charlie's feet thudded to the ground; air rushed from his lungs. "Malefactor," he said softly. "m-a-l-e-f-a-c-t-o-r."

The man stared at him dumbly.

"Malefactor," Charlie repeated. "M-A-L-E-F-A-C-T-O-R."

The man cupped a hand behind his ear. "Eh, what?"

"MALEFACTOR," shouted Charlie.

The man continued to stare at him. Exasperated, Charlie pulled a stub of pencil and his crumpled piece of paper from his pocket. "MALEFACTOR," he wrote in capital letters and passed it to his benchmate. The man smiled happily and returned to his puzzle.

"Malefactor...." mused Charlie. "An offender against the law. But then again," he continued, half to himself and half to anyone within earshot, "one must distinguish between criminal activity on the one hand and actions of conscience on the other. For example..."

In this manner, Charlie rambled on for nearly an hour with his views on corporate America (evil), high technology (equally evil), greed (the root of ALL evil), and the moral imperative for Significant Action to the contrary. On this last count, Charlie supplied specific examples, one specific example in particular, complete with rationale and details. His words fell on deaf ears; Charlie's companion remained engrossed in his puzzle.

Had Charlie been less engrossed in his own thoughts and more alert to the world around him, to the swirling bits of litter in particular, he might have noticed the crumpled scrap of paper that wafted from his benchmate's lap and settled inconspicuously between a crushed beer can and a soggy pair of panties, abandoned in the shrubbery.

In the distance, a familiar church clock chimed. Three o'clock. Jesus, he'd lost track of the time. Better get moving. Call Molly again – get that squared away. Get something to eat, too. "Keep the newspaper," he called to the figure hunkered at the farthest reach of the bench.

"Molly, Molly, Molly," chanted Charlie as he neared the phone booth. He recalled the anti-nuclear rally where he'd met her and told her his plan. And, whatever she'd thought of his plan – at one point she'd told him he was crazy, but that was her problem, not his – she *had* said he could stay at her place any time he needed it. So, this was going to blow her mind, core meltdown, so to speak. Charlie smiled at his own cleverness. And he began humming to himself at the thought of Molly. Not only was she properly aligned politically speaking, but she was cute and sexy to boot. In fact, politics were far from Charlie's mind by the time he reached into his pocket for Molly's phone number, searched frantically in his pocket for the crumpled scrap of paper. Then it hit him. Oh, Jesus – the wino! Malefactor!

Charlie turned on his heel and raced back to the park. Oh, Christ – the wino was gone! Distantly, out of the corner of his mind, Charlie remembered the scrap of paper fluttering away into the shrubbery. Searching wildly on his hands and knees, he clawed through the litter. Styrofoam cups, gum wrappers, pop-tops, condoms, hotdog wrappers...

"Looking for something, Buster?"

Charlie groaned. Same voice, same grating quality. His mind reeled, then settled. Grasping at straws – not to mention cups, wrappers, and pop-tops – he emerged from the shrubbery with an armload of litter." "Pigs," he said to Patrolman #836, shaking his head in disgust. "People just don't seem to care anymore." Clucking indignantly, he headed for the nearest trash can. Behind him, the nightstick smacked loudly and rhythmically. Charlie did not look back. He did not even breathe freely until he was clear of the park and back at the Sears store, staring through the window at a little Sony 500 TV with an afternoon game show flashing back at him.

By this point in his day, Charlie's mind, never altogether clear in the first place, had grown a little fuzzy around the edges. He half-expected to see himself on the Sony, hooting and cheering with the game show audience. As he stood watching, two dim thoughts crossed his mind. First, it was critically important that he watch the evening news. Second, it was just as important that he get in touch with Molly as soon as possible. No problem with the evening news; that was why he was here at Sears. But, how to get in touch with Molly? She wasn't listed in the phone book; he had lost the number she had given him.

Something caught Charlie's eye, a little Westinghouse just to the left of the Sony, a public service message. "For more information, call..."

Information! That was it! They'd have Molly's number, and he could take it from there. He'd wait until after the news, and he's call Molly then. More dramatic that way, especially if she had watched the news herself. Charlie's spirits soared as he entered the store and stood engrossed in the game show.

Until, suddenly, gliding from the shadows, a salesfigure to deal with. "May I help you find something, sir?" Exaggerated bobbing of head and wringing of hands.

But, by now, Charlie had gathered his wits and was back in charge. "Um, I don't think so," he said, stroking his chin thoughtfully. "Then again, I only judge a set by the news. There hasn't been any of that on this afternoon, has there? Bulletins? Special reports?"

"I'm sorry, Sir, nothing like that. Only the usual: soaps, game shows, Tarzan movies. The news runs from six until seven. Half an hour of local, then national."

"I see, I see," mused Charlie. "Perhaps I'll return then."

"That would be splendid, sir. Just ask for Roger; that's me."

Charlie liked dealing with Roger – no bulging T-shirt, no badge, no thwacking nightstick. He left the store whistling and rubbing his hands together. Oh, it was all coming together now. Couple of hours to kill. They'd probably have special reports on throughout the evening. Just cuddle up on the couch with Molly and – oh, this was going to be splendid.

Charlie did not return to his park. For the next few hours, he wandered the streets, munching on a fresh handful of hot-dogs and sipping Coca-Cola. By 5:45, he was back at Sears, in the Stationery Department, checking out cards for Molly. Through the cut-out heart of a Valentine's card, he could see Roger, carpet sweeping his department like a man with a treasure detector. Inside the card, what looked like a pigeon on the wing carried a removable, heart-shaped piece of candy in its beak. "Roses are red," the card said, "violet's are blue. My heart's beating fast, a-winging to you." Charlie pocketed the card and sauntered across the aisle.

With minutes to go now, Charlie patrolled the by-ways of Roger's world. Eighty-seven television sets he counted, twelve different brands, tuned to twenty-three different channels. He chose a spot where he could watch three major networks and placed a beige, plastic bucket chair accordingly. This was it. Countdown. The moment of truth.

Eyes darting from screen to screen, Charlie hunkered in his chair. Behind him, the hum of Roger's treasure detector grew closer.

"Ah, you're back," chirped Roger, abandoning his machine and rubbing his fingers under Charlie's nose. "May I say, sir, that the Quasar is an ex..."

"Shhh," hissed Charlie.

Roger bowed obsequiously. "Of course, of course, Sir, whatever you wish." He reached for his carpet-sweeper. "Oh my, oh my goodness!" Half a store away, trailing brassieres and panty-hose, Roger's machine was cruising towards Housewares. Roger initiated pursuit. "Oh my, oh my goodness."

Scornfully, Charlie turned away. Life's little farces and tragedies were far beneath him now. Intently, from the edge of his chair, he watched local anchormen, weathermen, and sportscasters cough politely and ape the motions of the network superstars. Elbows out, eyes earnest: "Good evening. This is (Jim or Jean or Peter Whomever) with your evening news..."

Charlie strained forward. "At the top of the news, state lawmakers propose more cutbacks in services to the..."

Charlie stared in disbelief. Top of the news?!

"Coming up, noted sports figure donates thousands..."

Followed by an Alpo dog food commercial.

Charlie struggled to gather his wits. His eyeballs ached. "Sheesh..." These local lightweights didn't know a top story when it blew up in their faces. Then again, maybe the news was being repressed; maybe officials didn't want this story out there where copycats abounded. But, no, by the onset of the daily Red Sox report, Charlie had returned to his original theory: the locals simply did not understand the significance of his action. The real appreciation would come from the major networks. Yeah, the national news was where it was at.

By the end of the local news, Charlie sat slouched in his chair, ashen-faced and quivery-lipped. He watched as the national newscasters shrugged and shouldered their way to full-screen close-up. It wasn't that he had given up hope – just that it had all taken on a surreal, dreamlike quality...

He jerked to attention. Suddenly... it was Dan Rather on CBS. "Act of political sabotage... daring night raid..."

Charlie was on his feet. Footage of flashing lights and milling crowds. Charlie squatting, nose-to-nose now with Barbara Walters.

"Sacramento police ... suspect in custody..."

Charlie staggered back. Wha?? Sacramento? Sacramento??? Suspect in cus... ?

Charlie collapsed in his chair. Glassy-eyed he watched as the story repeated itself from network to network. Mug shots of the suspect – young, frail looking. No way, no way! Charlie pounded his knees with his fists. The kid must be lying, hunting for headlines. You had to be strong, burning with conviction. This kid just didn't have it in him.

Deep inside, smothered under hot dogs and coffee, Joe's

breakfast began to churn in Charlie's stomach. His vision blurred. With his head between his knees, he heard the networks sign off, heard the hum of Roger's contraption approaching.

"Sir, sir, are you all right, sir?"

"Something I ate," gasped Charlie. Clutching his belly, he lurched from the store. Behind him, Roger's hand-wringing took on curious twists, as if he were practicing grips for the Heimlich Maneuver.

Outside, the night air caught Charlie like an uppercut. Stiff-backed and spastic, he wandered the streets like a punch-drunk fighter. Only one thought sustained him now – Molly. Yes, he would find Molly, and she would know what to do.

And one beacon. Yes, there at the end of a dark alley, there, his phone booth. All glass and chrome and bright light, there, hovering like a spacecraft, waiting to take him away.

Robot-like, Charlie approached the phone booth, circled twice with the moths, and entered. The metallic clang of the door, the clink of his quarter, the chigga-chigga of the dial, all echoed his feelings. With numbed expectations, Charlie dialed Information. "Adamson. Molly Adamson," he whispered into the mouthpiece.

"Claude, Hiram S., Xavier, no Molly," he repeated after the operator.

Charlie did not hang up. He slumped from the phone booth, leaving the receiver dangling on its cord. A tiny voice tinkled in the glassiness: "And a new listing, sir. For Arthur B. Sir? Sir?" But Charlie was long gone.

Hands pushed deep in his pockets, Charlie returned to his park. Fiddling with his fingers, he discovered the little candy heart on the Valentine's card in his pocket. Charlie lifted the little heart from its slot in the pigeon's mouth and popped it into his mouth. Numbly, in a position both pre-natal and pigeon-like, he perched on his park bench.

Strange images appeared, images of Molly, like a motorized doll, pushing Roger's machine through the shrubbery, sucking up litter and garbage. Behind her, unrolling like a carpet, America the Beautiful shone with promise. Overhead, pigeons fluttered about, clutching little candy hearts in their beaks...

Charlie blinked. Focus! Focus! He was falling apart here. What he needed now was to focus, to make a plan. Yes, that's what he needed – a plan. Whatever had gone before, only two doors were open to him now.

Charlie pondered his first option. He could stay where he was, risking certain arrest for vagrancy and a night in jail. He could see it all, the thwacking nightstick, his protestations of innocence, the cynical eyes and blinding lights, the old good cop / bad cop routine, no doubt, followed by his confession at last, blurted out with urgency and details galore. And what then? Charlie shuddered. What if they laughed, humored him along, and sent him packing on his way. What then?

Desperately now, Charlie pulled himself together, focused on his second option, focused on reality, for god's sake, *reality*. Face it, something was wrong – no Molly, nothing on the news, nighttime thickening – something was *wrong*. And there was only one thing to do about it, only one thing he *could* do about it – and that was to return to the turnpike and head south again, get back to the scene of The Action. He could see it now. Charlie closed his eyes, nourishing, embellishing.

"Planning on spending the night, Buster?" The voice grated. In the distance, church bells tolled eight.

Charlie did not look up, did not even open his eyes. One thought lodged in his mind, dominated his mind, and would not be moved: night and day, day and night, Patrolman #836 never went off duty. How do you deal with that? Charlie swallowed hard. End of little candy valentine heart, he noted.

(Author's note: The story, as written, ends here. As we suggested at the outset, Charlie is unstable at best, and the narrator a bit unreliable. Can this state of not-knowingness be the point of his story? A story about no-story? No one seems to know what came of Charlie that night on the park bench. There is an anecdotal report from a few years later that Charlie did in fact return to the scene of his "action," found nothing, and lived out his days in befuddled obscurity. Additionally, a short newspaper account appeared somewhere back then concerning a young boy on a bicycle finding a small, amateurish, homemade bomb unexploded in the shrubbery along the access road to the State's nuclear power plant in Wiscasset. As for the girl, Molly, a short story by a certain Molly Abramson appeared in an anthology a decade or so later. In that story, a young woman gives fake phone numbers and addresses to self-styled political activists who make unwanted advances at parties and protest marches. There is no provable linkage between the author Molly Abramson and the Molly of this story.)

THE STORY
OF THE UGLY SWEATER:
A GOOD MAINE YARN

The sweater, all later agreed, was really pretty awful – muddy beige with bands of red around the belly and biceps. It was purchased many years ago at a small used-clothing outlet, and it first shows up in a photograph of a child named Amanda at her fourth birthday party. Amanda appears to have many happy friends in the photograph, and she appears to be quite comfortable in the sweater. The sweater appears on Amanda in other pictures over the course of her childhood – not to mention pictures of her younger siblings.

No one seems to have noticed at the time a small tag inside the collar of the sweater – Property: Jason Furbish. Jason was presumably the original owner of the sweater, but there are to date no available pictures of young Jason in his sweater.

Amanda's sweater was purchased as part of a bag sale at a little shop on Main Street called Shop 'n Chat. Nobody knows for sure how Shop'n Chat came to be - reportedly as a mission of one of the churches oh so many years ago. It was a place where folks could buy clothing for pennies on the dollar. That was in the days before much fancier places, in fancier towns with Shoppes and Boutiques came to be – places where folks came to shop and drove off in Volvos and late model Subarus. At Shop-n Chat in those days, folks tended to drive off in pick-up trucks and old Chevies, heading home with bags full of clothing.

Back to our story. Time went by, as it does, and the

child Amanda outgrew her sweater. It next appears in a picture of her younger sister, Tiffany, at a Christmas party with cookie crumbs cascading from her chin. To this day, Tiffany hates that picture. "Did we ever go to a *real* store?" she asks her parents. But that WAS a real store, her dad points out. If an award were to be given out, he told them, (and perhaps it was) to the mission in the County that helped the greatest number of families and did it all with wisdom and kindness, doled out by twinkly-eyed women (mostly) who always found room for one more item in that all-you-can-fit-in-a-bag-for-a dollar sale, that award would have to go to Shop 'n Chat and all the saintly folks who worked there.

Dads do tend to hold forth. For all of that, the years rolled by, and Tiffany, like her sister, outgrew the sweater. It next appears on a boy, her cousin Arthur, a few years later. Arthur and his family have moved out of state by now. Arthur is smiling and holding a homemade bow and arrow. In another few years, the sweater will show up on his brother Jesse, cooking s'mores at a campfire somewhere over in Vermont.

And so on, through various birthing of siblings and cousins. What the sweater lacked in style and charm, it made up for in durability. And, as it made its way into the next generation, it gained a certain degree of historicity: "Your great uncle (or aunt) so-and-so wore that sweater." By that point, it had heirloom status, and no one dared to throw it out. It was always a source of great amusement to see yet another child wearing the sweater on Facebook or Instagram.

"Shop 'n Chat" the cousins would all recall with fond-ness and some forbearance, as if it were something out of

Mr. Rogers' Neighborhood. And if, as the years rolled by, more and more Volvos and Subarus could be found in the vicinity of the little shop, the owners of those cars tended, a bit furtively, to leave their cars out of sight behind a nearby flower shop.

And then, one rainy day in Boston many years later, a particularly inquisitive child asked the question dormant for so many years. She was looking at the name tag still sewn into the neck of the sweater. "Who is Jason Furbish?" she asked. Her mother took the sweater from her hand; she had never paid much attention to the name tag herself. "Hmmm," she mused. She fancied herself something of a family historian, and she promised to look into the matter.

Meanwhile, far away in Sacramento, a man, perhaps in his early sixties, was sorting through boxes of old papers and photographs. A young woman sat nearby, leafing through a large photo album. "Here's one you'll like, Dad" she said. In the picture, a young boy stood grinning widely. An empty box lay on the floor at his feet, and he was wearing a brownish sweater with red bands at the belly and biceps. A tag still dangled from the sleeve of the sweater. "I think that's you, Dad," the young woman said. "No wonder Mom divorced you. I wonder what ever came of that sweater?"

The man leaned over and peered at the picture. "I always hated that sweater," he said. "And it's not why your mother and I got divorced; in fact, your mother never saw the sweater. Your grandmother got rid of it when she moved us all to California – took it to that little shop the church ladies had back home in Maine..."

"Yuck," the young woman said. "Grammy told me about that place. I'm glad you moved to California."

Around the same time, back in Boston, the mother of the inquisitive child called her Auntie Amanda, recently moved back to Maine from Boulder, Colorado. "Auntie, do you remember that swea...?"

"Duh...could I ever forget?" She promised to go to Shop'n Chat the very next day to see what she could find out. She was recovering from a long and painful divorce in those days; she had recently moved back to her old hometown, and she welcomed this little adventure.

At Shop'n Chat the next day, Amanda found herself chatting with an elderly woman, who introduced herself as Phyllis. "Oh, yes, yes, yes," she said. "I went to school with Howard Furbish oh so long ago. Jason would have been his grandson. Jason and his parents moved to California when Jason was very young. I remember that because they brought bag after bag of clothes here for us to sort through. I even remember that sweater; it stayed on the shelf for the longest time before anyone took it home."

"Do you remember who it was that took it home?" Amanda asked. "Oh mercy no," Phyllis said. "It was one of those new families that moved in outback. Hippies, I think they were. They've all moved away now, too."

Amanda smiled and arched her eyebrows. She thanked Phyllis and went about her day. That night, just out of curiosity, she googled Jason Furbish.

"Dear Mr. Furbish," she wrote to an address she'd found in Sacramento. "I don't know if you remember me; you were years ahead of me in school. You were the cutest boy. You always wore this hideous sweater – muddy awful beige color with red bands all around it – as if you'd been grabbed by an octopus. I think I had a crush on you in those days. And then you moved away, and I was sad for weeks

73

on end. I was so happy when my mom came home with your old sweater..."

And so a correspondence began. "Wow," wrote Jason Furbish from Sacramento. "I do remember you. You were just a little kid, but you were pretty cute yourself. I've still got a lot of family up your way; my mom was like fourth generation; she thought your whole family were a bunch of newcomers – hippies, she called you."

That was in January, and the letters were emails by now. At first Amanda was offended at being dismissed as a hippie. And Jason felt a bit mischaracterized as some escaped local yokel. "Move a pig to California, it's still a pig," Amanda teased. And so the teasing continued – along with long accounts of the lives they'd led, their careers, former spouses, children. By February, they were signing their letters with terms of considerable fondness. By March, Jason was thinking that he might visit his old hometown sometime in the months ahead – just to reconnect with his family, mind you. But maybe the two of them might meet?

Meanwhile, behind the scenes, Jason's daughter – Beth is her name – was not oblivious to her father's brightening moods and occasional references to his new old friend back home in Maine. In fact, it might even be said that it was Beth who suggested the long overdue reunion with his family – not to mention his new friend. A careful observer might even have watched her snip a picture out of her dad's old photo album. And on subsequent visits to her father's home, that same observer might have noticed a colorful bag on the arm of the daughter – a bag with yarns and knitting needles – and a corner of that very snipped-out picture sticking out at the top....The ensuing months passed quickly. Letters flew back and forth. It was Amanda who first signed off "With GREAT Fondness..." In May, the first awkward and hesitant phone call was initiated by Jason from Sacramento. Years later, Amanda remembered especially liking the rich tone of his voice – though even at the beginning she raised her eyebrows a bit at the way he said "idear" instead of "idea".

Spring came differently to Maine and California, and by late May it was decided that Jason would come for his visit over the Fourth of July holidays in June. Both of them were retired from their jobs at this point, living on social security and pensions, and they were pretty much free to schedule their lives. It was even agreed that Amanda would meet Jason's plane at the airport up in Bangor, just to the north.

"But how will I recognize you?" Amanda had asked.

"Not to worry," Jason had answered. "I think Beth has taken care of that."

And so it came to pass. Nervous as a schoolgirl, Amanda waited by the gate at the airport. Passengers emerged, tall passengers, short passengers, men, women, passengers of different colors, and passengers with and without coats and hats and carry-off luggage.

And then suddenly a particular passenger emerged, a nondescript man, not tall or short, handsome or not, but with a great smile on his face and a certain enthusiasm about him. And he was wearing a sweater, an oversized, ugly sweater, muddy beige with red bands around the belly and biceps. Amanda's heart skipped a beat. She hesitated for a moment, then rushed to the man, found herself wrapped in the arms of this stranger she'd known most of her life.

In the months that followed, Jason and Amanda shared

many adventures and intimate moments. In the end, they decided to spend their lives together, living in a small condo in this town on the banks of the river. And just across the street from them and a few steps up the sidewalk, was the little shop where it all began.

As for the sweater, it was on their first night actually spent together that Amanda had discreetly lifted the collar and noticed the little tag: "Jason AND Amanda," it had said. It would be years before she would actually meet Beth, an architect in Sacramento and the architect of her current romance. And it would be more years before the sweater would find its way to the little shop just across the street – but that will be a different story.

Meanwhile, the original sweater, Jason's childhood sweater, was last spotted on a little dark-skinned boy playing stickball in an alley down in Boston. These sweaters last forever – something about the good Maine yarn they're made with.

DIARY OF A ROTO-TILLER

We are sitting on a back deck in Newport, Maine. Tom Garvey, recently retired from Garvey, Soper, and Morrison, Attorneys at Law in Newport, tells tales of a dozen or so of what he calls happy hippie households in the area in the 1970s. Tom and his wife, Joyce, were among them. Call them what you like, Tom says — hippies, disillusioned yuppies, urban and academic refugees, whatever. They were young families seeking an alternative lifestyle, and they were all well-versed in something called The Whole Earth Catalogue which shared space in every kitchen with Scott and Helen Nearing's *Living the Good Life*.

"We were all so serious back then," Tom says. He tells about folks who had never hammered a nail, milked a goat, or planted a zucchini. Not to mention raised long-haired children in school districts that didn't know quite what to make of them. But they worked hard – no one would deny that – and they lived by their beliefs. They respected and learned from the old-timers in the area. Their children did well in school, too, made friends easily. They even participated in something called the Green Grass Softball League, but that is a different story. If they could be faulted, according to Tom, it was more for an excess of zeal than anything else.

Tom enjoys illustrating that last point with a particular story. As he tells it, there were six families altogether involved in what he calls the great roto-tiller experiment. As Tom explains it, the idea of collaborating and sharing equipment was deeply rooted in a philosophy already shared by most of the families involved – a somewhat patchwork philosophy not always consistent within itself.

After all, for all the collaboration and shared idealism among these discrete households, they were, in fact, discrete households. Elsewhere in the country, all kinds of communal living situations were popping up, but not so among this group of back-to-the-landers in Maine. Some of them had talked about the concept back in the early days, but they were all too independent to hitch themselves to a common wagon and pull in the same direction. Which is not to say that they did not help each other out with roof-raisings, garden plantings, childcare, and so on. The idea of communalism was very much shared—it's just there was a limit. Relationships were monogamous for the most part, and financial resources were personal and rarely discussed—though it was bandied about at one point that someone named Emily had inherited partial ownership in an oil well in Oklahoma. Tom observes that, even way back then, those without property tended to ask such questions as, *What are we going to do about snowplowing in the wintertime?* While those who already owned property tended to ask, *What are you going to do about snowplowing in the wintertime?* Issues of ownership lurked in the shadows even at the outset.

Those early years rolled by, and it became inevitable that, at some point, someone was going to raise a particular question.

Frank and Emily were a young family from Illinois. Frank had been a high school math teacher, and Emily had just quit her job as a middle school guidance counselor. They were both pretty fed up with the parent culture, they called it, the military-industrial complex, such as it was, the ongoing war in a faraway Southeast Asian country. They'd come to Maine with their two young boys, a Whole Earth

Catalogue in hand, and plans to create a healthy, alternative, country life for their kids. They had already built a small shed-roofed house on ten acres of land they'd purchased with their savings. What little money they now needed, they earned by teaching courses at a regional Adult Education Center. Emily was passionate about education, about home-schooling her kids, about possibly building a small alternative school for *all* the happy hippie kids. And it was Emily who suggested at a gathering of friends and like-minded homesteaders that it was a bit wasteful for each home to be renting a roto-tiller every time they needed to turn over a garden, that it might make sense for folks to band together and purchase a community roto-tiller – within limits, of course. The idea fell on fertile soil, such as it was at the time. Discussion followed. Ownership would be shared, of course – no question about that, but it would be structured in such a way as to ensure individual responsibility and accountability. These folks were all savvy enough by this point to understand the finicky nature of machinery, not to mention the differing skill sets enjoyed variously among themselves.

Roger, for example, was an excellent mechanic and could always be counted on for advice on a spluttering carburetor or faulty windmill blade. He and his wife Jocylyn had come from careers in Rhode Island and had built a small pottery studio for her while living in a tent and gathering materials for the house they would build. Roger was well aware of his skills and his usefulness to the community-at-large and had grown a bit protective of his time. It was Roger who suggested that a notebook be created and be kept with the tiller at all times. At ALL times, Roger repeated.

Tom chuckles at his recollections. Someone named Amber, he recalls, along with her partner Aubry, were a bit put off by the suggestion of a notebook. Couldn't we all just trust each other, after all? Of all the families involved, Aubry and Amber lived the most communally, sharing as they did a plot of land with another couple, Bill and Mika. Aubry raised large sheep dogs and knew more about organic gardening than anyone in the group. They all shared a huge old farmhouse that was often overflowing with wanderers and passersby. Little tents dotted the meadow behind the house, and spritely young women could often be spotted working bare-breasted in their gardens. Aubry thought he might have an old unused notebook that might serve as The Book, as he called it, but the discussion veered elsewhere at that point.

As he tells the story, it was Tom Garvey himself who then jumped in, pointing out the practical, possibly even legal, benefits of a notebook, a kind of journal, that passed from household to household with the tiller. After all, he'd pointed out, if the tiller required an oil change every eighteen hours of use, for example, how would anyone know when and how to make that happen, if no records were kept of the usage?

Whereupon Mika (not really part of the discussion), had wondered why the oil needed changing in the first place. Wasn't that part of the military-industrial conspiracy we were all trying to get away from?

Here, Tom remembers Roger sighing deeply and re-joining the conversation. He was really busy building a new goat shed out behind his house, but he would host a little training session on essential care and maintenance of a Troy-Bilt roto-tiller. Once it was decided, of course, that money would be pooled and it would in fact be a Troy-Bilt purchased – a no-brainer, of course, because that was the Number One recommendation in the Whole Earth Catalogue. In addition, Roger would take responsibility, once a notebook design, format, and color had been decided upon – and thank you Aubry for your kind offer of a ratty old notebook - for creating a cover page with basic, most pertinent information. That page would include simple instructions on how and when to service the engine along with a reminder to keep attached AT ALL TIMES the Service Manual provided by the manufacturer – presumably Troy-Bilt, unless, of course, the group (he did not say stupidly) decided otherwise. Subsequent pages would be for regular recordings of problems, maintenance done, and any concerns about the condition of the tiller. Most important, hours of usage would be recorded exactly, and routine maintenance would be done accordingly. Roger himself would offer a training at the outset around care and maintenance of the tiller. If everyone was okay with that...

Here someone named Mindy – Tom has fond memories of Mindy – entered the discussion. Darla and Mindy were architects from Philadelphia. They designed earth-bermed houses around the County and practiced their own alternative lifestyle on the side of a mountain out at Babcock Corners. As a team, Darla specialized in most of the engineering and site work, and Mindy was responsible for design – both interior and exterior. It was Mindy who offered to dig through her boxes of materials for a finely-bound blank book that she had brought from Philadelphia. After much group discussion, it was decided that this book would be kept in a waterproof bag (along with the official

Troy-Bilt manual) that was to accompany the tiller everywhere it went. That was EVERYWHERE it went, Roger reminded the group. And it was Mindy who offered to dig out her official calligraphy set and indelibly letter on the front of the book: *THE BOOK,* as it was now officially dubbed. (As Tom Garvey remembers the voting, there were two nay votes and one abstention.)

Tom pauses at this point in his story, disappears into his owner-built, timber-peg house, and returns with two bottles of homebrew. We are sitting on his porch, as I mentioned, overlooking a lush vegetable garden (all very organic) and a small pasture full of bleating goats. All these years later, Tom still clings to remnants of his life back then.

Tom pours the homebrew carefully into glasses, careful not to disturb the sediment in the bottles. There were five families involved altogether in the great, Troy-Bilt roto-tiller saga, he repeats. He's already talked about some of them, he says, but to summarize briefly:

Family #1: There was his own family, of course. Tom himself had been a schoolteacher and was working at the time as an assistant to a well-driller. His wife Joyce was a respiratory therapist and together they had moved from New Jersey and were living in a yurt built in a meadow surrounded by forest. They had two children at the time, ages one and three, and weren't sure whether to homeschool them or work with the local school system. Perhaps Emily had some ideas? It wouldn't be until five years later that Tom would return to school, get his law degree, and set up practice in Newport with old-timers, Orville Soper and Charlie Morrison.

Family #2: Frank and Emily. He's already talked about

Frank and Emily, and, yes, it was Emily who suggested this whole idea of a shared tiller in the first place. Her gardens, wholly organic and regularly tended with Frank at her side, were the most visually stunning of all. It was her dream to have gardening, flowers along with produce, a major component of the curriculum at her school.

Family #3: Roger and Jocylyn. Again, he's already talked about Roger and Josie, as folks called her. Josie did very well with her pottery, having brought a large mail-order clientele with her from Rhode Island. As it turned out, Roger's tiller-training was excellent; it turned into a potluck supper and barn dance later in the evening. His meticulously cut-and-pasted roto-tiller maintenance plan became an indispensable tool in the days and months that followed.

Family #4: Aubry and Amber and their entourage. For all his gardening expertise and zen-master demeanor, Aubry had been the most politically active of the group, claiming to have been involved in the bombing of a research center in San Diego. Bill and Mika were beyond doubt the biggest potheads of the group, spending as they did most of their time in a little cannabis patch they cultivated out behind the toolshed. Others worried a bit about the image they projected to the townsfolk a few miles away. They were not part of the tiller collective as Tom Garvey referred to it at one point. (Even back then, I'm told by others involved, Tom was known for a certain arching of eyebrows and tendency towards irony in his pronouncements.)

Family #5 – Michael and Paula and their three children were not at the original meeting. They were transplants from elsewhere like everyone else, and they were avid students of The Whole Earth Catalogue. They were out working in their gardens one day when visitors appeared cheerfully at the gate. The visitors wore white shirts and shiny black shoes. When they left, Paula held a handful of leaflets and was sold on their message. After that, she and her family could no longer attend community events, especially those with pagan rituals or symbols. But they stayed in touch with their old friends. Michael especially enjoyed talking with Emily and others about education for the children – especially where home-schooling was involved. As far

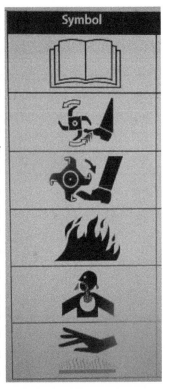

Symbol

as the roto-tiller went, there was nothing pagan about a roto-tiller, especially a Troy-Bilt roto-tiller. Michael and Paula were enthusiastic participants in the enterprise of the roto-tiller.

Here again, Tom pauses in the telling of his story. Here again he disappears into his house, craftily constructed and replacing the yurt of the early years. He appears again with two fresh bottles of his acclaimed homebrew. Prosit, he offers. He is also carrying a book. Still intact and obviously once beautifully bound, it is worn, scarred, weathered, and mangled at the corners. In faded script across the front, the lettering is still discernable: *THE BOOK*. Shadows are settling over the gardens below. Someone is down milking goats in the barn. Tom turns on a light behind me and urges me to look through the pages.

Yes, the title is still discernable: *THE BOOK*. And, as promised, Roger had placed dire warnings on the very first page. This was serious business, no game at all for Roger.

CARE AND USE OF TROY-BILT BRONCO ROTO-TILLER

(Copies of this document to be signed and dated by all parties involved.)

WARNING: DO NOT PUT HANDS OR FEET NEAR ROTATING PARTS. CONTACT WITH ROTATING PARTS CAN AMPUTATE HANDS AND FEET. FAILURE TO OBSERVE SAFETY INSTRUCTIONS COULD RESULT IN SERIOUS INJURY OR DEATH!

WARNING #2: FAILURE TO MAINTAIN OIL LEVEL AND CHANGE AT APPROPRIATE INTERVALS COULD RESULT IN CRITICAL DAMAGE OR DEATH OF MACHINE. PLEASE REPORT ALL CONCERNS AND HOURS OF USAGE IN THIS BOOK.

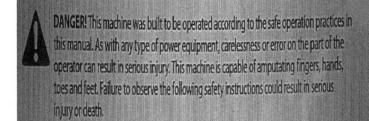

DANGER! This machine was built to be operated according to the safe operation practices in this manual. As with any type of power equipment, carelessness or error on the part of the operator can result in serious injury. This machine is capable of amputating fingers, hands, toes and feet. Failure to observe the following safety instructions could result in serious injury or death.

Maintenance Schedule

	Check After first 2 hours	Before each use	Every 5 Hours	Every 10 Hours	Every 30 Hours	See Engine Manual
Check Motor Oil Level		✓	✓			
Clean Engine		✓				✓
Check Drive Belt Tension	✓			✓		
Check Nuts and Bolts	✓			✓		
Lubricate Tiller				✓		
Check Gear Oil Level in Transmission					✓	
Check Tines for Wear					✓	
Check Air Pressure in Tires					✓	

Technically, Tom points out all these years later, that was not a legal document, though all parties dutifully signed copies. It did tend to absolve Roger of any sense of responsibility for damages suffered or inflicted.

I thumb through the pages of *THE BOOK*. Entries from that first spring are glowing and full of energy and enthusiasm.

May 22, 1975. Frank & Emily. *Tiller is great! Fluffy soil. One hour and twenty minutes of use. Does anyone have any cucumber sets?*

May 26, 1975. Darla & Mindy. *Fantastic. Thanks to Emily for this great idea. Thanks to Roger for the training. Two hours of use. No cucumbers; I do have some cilantro.*

June 4, 1975. Aubry & Amber. *Amber speaking. Aubry tilled for exactly two hours. I'm scared to use it. Yes, we have some cukes. And what are these little black flies everywhere. They're awful. PEACE everyone.*

And so it goes through that first burst of springtime euphoria. Even Roger wrote in thanking everyone for their great efforts, while recording four hours of tiller use for himself. And it was Tom's own partner, Joyce, who wrote back noting two hours and ten minutes of tilling time and thanking Roger again for the far out training he had done for them all.

"Far out training..." Tom chuckles and continues his narrative. By September, all the households brought produce to a large farmer's market. Sales were great, in October, they got together for a wildly successful harvest festival. Jottings in *THE BOOK* are cheery and hopeful; helpful hints about putting gardens to bed and getting through the winter are scrawled in the margins. All is grooviness and harmony – just a few small suggestions of anything less:

Sept. 26, 1975. Frank & Emily. *Thanks, Darla, for dropping the tiller off. Two hours of use. Changed oil and tightened belts. Two things: there was Miracle-Gro in the crud on the tines. Do not use that in your garden. And please clean tines before passing tiller along. I do not want your shit in my garden. (P.S. Emily would kill me for writing this.)*

Sept. 27, 1975. Michael & Pauls. *Paula here. Michael tilled for two hours and eight minutes. Soil looks great. I TOLD him to remove all rocks before tilling, but he hit one anyway. It makes me so mad. But the tines look okay. Praise the Lord.*

Sept. 29, 1975. Roger. *Josie is off visiting her parents in Rhode Island. That tine is definitely bent. Will need replacing. I need two people to help me take the tiller in for routine maintenance. Volunteers?*

Praise the Lord, indeed. According to Tom Garvey, all households involved made it through the following winter. With the tiller project still nascent, it was decided to hold off on the idea of a collaboratively owned snowblower. Again, that arching of Tom's eyebrows.

By springtime again, he continues, folks were building

polyethylene greenhouses and placing large orders with Johnny's Selected Seeds. The tiller wintered well in a little shelter Roger had built for it out behind Josie's pottery shed. Once again, entries in *THE BOOK* became glowing and enthusiastic. Issues of picking-up and dropping-off had been well resolved the year before. The damaged tine had been replaced during annual maintenance – though Roger insisted he could have done it himself. *THE BOOK* itself was getting a little beaten up but remained in good shape and had many blank pages – like long furrowed rows waiting for seeds. All households involved appeared to have survived the winter. Now, as Tom Garvey fetches another round of homebrew, not to mention some goat cheese and crackers, I continue my browsing.

"Lots of cheerful entries here," I tell Tom. "Sounds like everyone got their gardens tilled okay. Oh," I exclaim. "Here's a note from you, Tom."

May 26, 1976. Tom & Joyce. *Tiller running great! Two and a half hours of use. But, hey, guys, just a heads-up. Here's something that really pisses me off – when one of you (not to mention any names) uses the tiller right up until two minutes before oil-change time and then drops it off for the next user (me!) to deal with. JESUS! Just till your garden for another two minutes and CHANGE THE FUCKING OIL! OK?*

May 28, 1976. Michael & Paula. *Just one hour of tilling. Machine running good. Could we please refrain from taking the name of the Lord in vain in this journal?*

May 29, 1976. Aubry & Amber. *Amber speaking. Four hours of tilling. Aubry does the tilling; I'd cut my foot off. Here's a poem I wrote:* **My toes and fingers I do need / Roger's warning I will heed.** *Also, Mika wants to know if* she can use Troy. *(Okay if I call it Troy? I used to know a Troy who sounded like that when he snored.) She needs it to do her Mary Jane patch. Here's a poem she wrote,* **Here comes the tiller, oh my god / We finally get to move this sod.**

June 4, 1976. Darla & Mindy. *Just thirty minutes of tilling. We did our own little garden. It's so steep! Does anyone mind if Mindy uses the tiller for some landscaping she does for a client?*

June 6, 1976. Frank & Emily. *Emily speaking. Frank used the tiller for three hours. He tells me belts and oil are all okay. I think we need to go over the rules. In my school, I will teach children that when we make an agreement, we need to stick to it. And we all agreed that the tiller was ONLY for our own use – not to be shared or lent out.*

Following that entry, as Tom recalls, a general meeting of owners was called and it was agreed that Mindy's client and Mika could NOT use the tiller. (Tom himself, as he recalls, supported this decision from a legal standpoint, unschooled as he was in such matters at the time.) Also, entries in *THE BOOK* would be limited to basic information about the tiller and its usage. Poetic impulses and flowery observations could express themselves elsewhere. Four of the women at the meeting objected to this caveat. Roger reminded everyone that it was a huge NO-NO to ever pass the tiller along with anything less than a full tank of gas. .

In the course of the ensuing summer and fall, entries in *THE BOOK* are terse and to-the-point – with one or two notable exceptions.

September 17, Michael & Darla. *Darla speaking. Please do NOT leave weeds tangled in the tines of the tiller! Our gardens reflect a struggle between the forces of good and the agents of evil. Please keep your weeds to yourself. Two hours of use (and I did it all). Praise the Lord.*

October 5, 1976. Aubry and Amber. *Amber speaking. Aubry just tilled up the big garden. Three hours. He says his elbow hurts. I know we're not supposed to write poetry, but Mika asked me to share this (she's pissed that we won't let her use the tiller):* **Whatever happened to the hoe? / No gas required to make it go. / No fossil fuel for me today - / Pitchfork and rake will clear the way.**

October 15, 1976. Roger & Josie. *One hour and forty-five minutes of use. Note to all: STOP MESSING WITH THE IDLER ADJUSTMENT. I will adjust when necessary. I could use some help again with annual maintenance and storage for the Winter. Volunteers? (P.S. Just for the record: a pitchfork is for hay time. You want a spading fork for your garden.)*

In the course of that second winter—again, according to Tom's recollections—it became tacitly understood that the "spirit" of the collaboration had become a bit compromised. A general meeting was called and, with Emily once again the driving force, it was decided that some changes would be made, some fundamental changes. In the future, the men would do the physical labor and the women would handle all else—the record-keeping, the seed-ordering, the planning of the gardens. That went against the general understanding of gender equity, but it seemed to make sense in terms of getting the work done and maintaining harmony. Only Darla and Mindy objected to the changes, and a general exception was made in their case.

That spring, zinnias and marigolds were planted along with root crops and vegetables. Three new babies were born with gender and weight recorded in *THE BOOK*.

Gardens flourished, and the Festival that fall was greater than ever. By late fall, however, certain problems arose.

Sept. 26, 1976. Darla. *Just me and the kid now. No more Michael. I think he didn't like the cold. And, just between you and me, I think he was faking being saved. Good riddance. I can run this damn tiller by myself. Two hours of use. Praise the Lord.*

Praise the Lord, indeed, grins Tom. Shortly after that, Paula abandoned her stake in the tiller altogether, finding it more convenient to use the machine already owned by her religious community.

Then, to the dismay of everyone, an all but fatal blow: Mindy decided she needed her own tiller for her burgeoning landscape business. She asked the collaborative, such as it was, to pony up her one-sixth share of the original investment – less minor depreciation, that was.

Make that major depreciation, countered Roger. And that's when the collaborative enthusiasm really began to waver and wane. Long discussions ensued, and the role of filthy lucre became a dominant issue. Who owed whom what? And it wasn't long after that that Roger himself became exasperated and gave, gratis, his share back to the group. He tore up his copy of the original agreement and burned it in his Ashley Wood-burning Stove. That was the death knell, as Tom Garvey tells the story. He shakes his head. Filthy lucre, indeed...That agreement wasn't even a legal document.

And that was pretty much the end of the roto-tiller experiment. Over the course of that next winter, Frank and Emily pulled up stakes and moved back to traditional jobs and warmer climates. No one knew quite where the tiller spent that winter, but by springtime, folks had gone back to renting smaller, front-end tillers from Jerry's Garden Equipment and Supplies, where there was no maintenance to worry about and no one to complain about oil changes and Miracle-Gro on the tines. Not to mention who owed whom how much money.

By this point in the evening, Tom Garvey and I are both a bit tipsy from his homebrew. The book lies open in my lap, the final entry from Roger.

October 17, 1976. *No hours of use. Tiller's in the shop. Sorry guys; I can't do this anymore. Followed by a whole lot of empty pages.*

I put *THE BOOK* back on the table. Across the meadow, in the deepening shadows, I notice the outline of a tiller – familiar Troy shape—half-hidden in the alders. "Is that it?" I ask. Tom Garvey grins again, mumbles something about ownership by default.

Behind the tiller, tangled in the alders, an old Volkswagen microbus squats on its wheel hubs. A forty-foot maple tree grows up through the floorboards and out through the sunroof.

PART II –
THEM FOLKS OUTBACK:
A WHOLE LOTTA HONEY

(Note: The concept of Outback is a bit murky. I think of John Berger's long study, *Pig Earth,* about the transition in France from an agrarian model to a more urban, industrial model. Up here in Maine (and elsewhere, I'm sure), a distinct *outback* way of life persists, a certain do-it-yourself approach, a certain caginess around the code enforcers from town. Over the years, I have scribbled down random notes—glimpses and snatches of that life as I have witnessed it.)

OLD HENRY

There were so many stories back then, always with one Old Henry or another, be it Henry or Leo or Wilbur—or even one of the womenfolk, the wives and housemates of the men who got all the attention.

Many of the stories were gathered by young people, "outlanders" to Henry, returning to the land, building houses, raising organic vegetables—and children. This wave of enthusiasm was welcomed by the old-timers; their own offspring had long since departed for greener pastures.

So eager to learn these young people were. So sincere and well-intentioned. So principled and driven by ideals. They worshipped such gods on their pedestals as Truth, Beauty, Art, Ecology...

Old Henry would snort. He had long since put away his childish things (such as they were). If he had a goddess of Playfulness, she occupied an old milking stool, neglected, out behind the woodshed. In Henry's pantheon, the overarching god, towering over all others, scowling from his ten-foot pine stump pedestal, was Blister, Lord Supreme of WORK. And, in the end, of course, that's what Old Henry came to appreciate about the newcomers: they worked hard, worked until sunset, worked until their fingers were raw.

What's more, it was *him,* Old Henry, they were eager to learn from. They built chimneys and timber-frame barns. They hand-dug wells and hauled firewood from the forest. They built playgrounds for their children. And they did it all under the watchful, guiding, mocking, and twinkling eye of Old Henry. Even the children were kinda cute; Henry had to admit that. Who was to notice as the years went by if that neglected little figure out behind Henry's woodshed edged a bit out of the shadows?

Meanwhile, back in towns, the Councils were meeting regularly, the Chambers of Commerce scratched their heads, and the ladies of the Garden Clubs, looked up "organic" in their dictionaries. A famous folksinger wrote a song about how the times they were a'changin', and little weekly newspapers wrote editorials about hippies moving in, buying up the land, selling marijuana to school children on the playground.

That's when Old Henry's eyes really twinkled. He knew something about townsfolk, how they liked to regulate stuff. He'd had his own battles over the years. He knew something about that wacky-weed, too, had his own little patch, just down past the deer stand in his woodlot. No harm in that. What he liked most about these new folks movin' in was the way they didn't care much one way or t'other about what the townsfolk might think. They did things their own way – just like him.

Like Molly, too, for that matter, his wife and partner of fifty years. Dark-skinned she was, from one of the Wabanaki tribes, married to Old Henry, fourth generation Mainer but newcomer to her People of the Dawn. Side by side in the woods they worked, harvesting timber year after year behind their big team of horses. Until one winter— Molly was eighty years old then, Henry a few years older— Molly slipped on the ice, slipped under the great cleated hooves of the horses. Iron spikes raked down the back of her leg, stripping the flesh from the bone. Old Henry did the best that he could, got the horses to the barn, got Molly to the truck, got the truck to the hospital, where the doctors did all that they could. After four days, *Gotta amputate the leg*, the doctors said. *No way*, Molly said, and Wilbur got Molly to the truck, got the truck back home, got Molly to their bed, where he slathered her leg in Blue Lightning Horse Liniment. *Healed it up pretty good too,* according to Molly a few years later. After three weeks, she was limping around on her own, and a few weeks after that, she was back in the woods again, working with Henry behind the big team of horses. In telling the story afterwards, she would hike up her long skirt and show you the back of her leg, like a rutted tote road, all gouged and furrowed in mud season. She'd quit working in the woods a few years after that, she would say. She was eighty-six,;Henry a few years older. The leg was fine, she would tell you; it was her back that wore out.

Today, Old Henry is long gone, and Molly died a few years after him. The newcomers they nurtured and welcomed are old-timers themselves now, with newer newcomers seeking their advice. Old Henry's legacy lives on. Townsfolk continue to scratch their heads, make new regulations. Code Enforcement Officers lie awake at night, unlist their phone numbers, encourage their own kids to go into a different line of work. Deep in his grave, Old Henry rolls over, sighs contentedly. His work is done, and Blister is safe on his pedestal.

THEM FOLKS OUTBACK

Author's Note: The following thirteen sketches are gleaned from the aforementioned "scribbled notes." These glimpses of outback life as I have witnessed it, recorded in hopes of honoring that life and the characters involved.

WALTER'S CAVE

Towering boulders, domed at the tops, and, lower down, a great slab of granite between them. That was Walter's cave, according to my brother, who was guiding us down the flank of Groundhog Hill yesterday in search of our Christmas greenery.

Walter use t'live down at the foot of the hill, he would tell you. Played cat'n mouse when the game wardens come lookin' for him.

Walter was schooled in that kind of thing. Eyes twinkled when he told his stories. As a boy, he'd had an old wood-stove in the cave. Use t'camp out there, even in the wintertime.

This was storybook stuff, my brother said, like something you'd read about as a kid. Even do as a kid. After all, we'd camped in the woods, too, built lean-tos and shot at crows with our sling shots and BB guns.

But that was all make-believe compared to Walter's adventures. We never brought home venison, jacked deer out of season to feed our families through the winter. Or baited bears for whatever that was all about.

And yesterday, standing in the corner, we were humbled and hushed. And we trudged from the forest, erasing our tracks with the fir boughs we dragged behind us.

TOUGH AS NAILS

Tough as nails she was. Arlene Bost we're talking about, wiry and strong as an ox, hacking at the soil in her gardens, lugging buckets of topsoil and horseshit from one ramshackle greenhouse to another, face smudged, brown from the sun. Child strapped to her hip. Raising him by herself she was, along with organic vegetables for the folks in town.

In the winter, she'd clean houses for those same folks in town, scrape scraps of her own rutabaga from splashboards over their sinks. She was a good worker, folks said, and honest as the day was long. She raised her son to be a fine young man. He played tackle for his high school football team and went on to marry one of the Smith girls and raise three fine children of his own. He was a doting father, folks say, and a good worker, honest as the day was long.

No one knows what ever became of his mother. Just disappeared one day way back then. Her greenhouses collapsed, gave way to the brambles.

The Fire Department used her old house for a practice burn. Folks say her boy was the Volunteer who did the torching. But no one knows that for sure...

THE OLD SIGNPAINTER

People say he used to paint signs for a living. Was good at it, too... Could probably have had a career painting pictures for people – mountains, trees, birds, even a tractor in a field, with cattle under an oak tree.

But not now... Drink got to him, people say. Hands too shaky for painting letters or feathers on the wing of a bird.

You can see him walking down roads now, outback there, picking up cans and bottles, even litter, just to do his part, then shuffling his way home, home to a little shack, ramshackle, in the woods along the old Church Road. Outback.

Home... with sagging floors, and a rusted tricycle in the dooryard.

Home with a mural painted on the north wall, outside, where the old man can see it from his outhouse. A subtle and evocative picture of a pasture just up the road, cattle grazing under an oak tree, old John Deere tractor, abandoned nearby.

The picture, touched-up just yesterday, and brilliant in the late-afternoon light, fades into the forest now, as the sun sets behind the mountain, and darkness creeps through the valley.

WHOLE LOTTA HONEY

Horace McGinn showed up on my porch one day. He'd lined a bee, he said, five miles through the woods from his house to a split-trunked hemlock down by the brook on the far end of my property. He wanted permission to cut the tree down, get the honey.

Horace lived off the land, always had, one way or t'other, he would tell you. I followed him through the woods, maybe half a mile to the tree he'd found, a magnificent hemlock on the banks of the brook. Eight foot split down the center of the trunk. Thousands of bees buzzing about and birds twittering in the branches. Little brook babbling underneath.

Lotta honey in there, Horace said. *Whole lotta honey...*

I shook my head, imagined the tree crashing down, chaos in the forest. I didn't even speak.

I know, I know, Horace said. *Can't say I disagree with you. Just wanted you t'see somethin' special...*

BACKWOODS JUSTICE

Old Millard Gray out there, one of a kind, story after story about the old days, about gaming the game warden, gaming the system. Said he was unfit for service back in the First Big War. Told the sergeant he could shoot the eye out of a squirrel from half a mile away. Would never aim his gun at living human being,

Last week, Millard's old neighbor Hal showed up, shaking his head, eyebrows singed to his bony brow.

Jeezum Criminy, he'd said to Millard. *Never seen the like of it. Log blew up in my wood-stove. Blew a hole clean through the chimbly.*

Millard clucked solicitously. He'd sort of suspected it was Hal, absconding with a log every now and then from the top of his woodpile. So he'd gone out secretive like, and drilled holes in the butt ends of some logs, them that was most handy. Filled 'em with gunpowder and plugged 'em up so neat no one would ever notice. Figgered he'd find out soon enough who it was stealin' his logs.

I sorta suspected it was Hal, old Millard said afterwards. *Otherwise, I woulda used dynamite.*

THAT GRIZZLED OLD FART

That grizzled Old Fart at the gas pumps, Willard's Country Store, it was called, little mom & pop place. You could buy fishing worms inside.

One time, pouring rain, Old Fart pumping gas, customer asking, *Think it'll stop raining?*

Old Fart capping the tank, pausing for full effect, drawling, *Usually does.*

Customer shaking his head. *Think we'll get a frost tonight?*

Yup... iff'n it gets cold enough."

'Nother time, young couple with a new baby, just coming home from the hospital. Old Fart peering into the car, marveling, *Now ain't she a cunnin' little bugger.*

Young couple beaming. Old Fart, eyes clouded with cataracts, tears on his cheeks, shaking his head in wonderment.

THE OLD PAISLEY TIE

What a wild man he was, this Eddy Ormsby, crazy on his Harley, racing down the roads at Hagan's Corners. Worked in the woods too, worked with his wife Penelope. (What a beauty she was, from New York folks said, dancing so fiercely with her husband at neighborhood gatherings.) They worked together in the woods with their big work horse, their big workhorse named Donk.

Once at a neighborhood gathering, Ed admired a tie I was wearing, paisley and knotted at the neck. *Here*, I said, and gave him the tie. For months after that, he wore it as a headband. *Kept the sweat from his eyes,* he said. Until one day the halter broke at Donk's cheekbone, and Ed fixed it with my old paisley tie.

Two nights after that, Donk wandered out of his stall, wandered into the road at Hagan's Corners, and was hit by a man named Jules driving too fast in his Jeep. And it fell upon Ed to put Donk out of his misery with a single shot from his deer rifle.

Donk was buried the next day. Ed delivered a seven-word eulogy. *There's an empty stall in my heart,* was all he said.

Two weeks later, Ed's motorcycle skidded on the loose gravel at Hagan's Corners, and Ed was killed in the accident. We sprinkled his ashes near Donk's grave on the back of Ragged Mountain. The pellets pelted like hail on the dry autumn leaves. Nearby, someone had hung the paisley tie from the branch of a tree.

MIRACLE WORKER

Old Gladys set the brake on her wheelchair. *That's how they done it back then,* she explained. She'd been settin' down by the river way back then, and, just up to the landing, she'd seen her old neighbor Mabel come down and put something in the water. Turns out, it was a litter of kittens, eyes not even open. *That's how they done it back then,* she said again. And she felt sorry for them kittens, plucked them from the river, and that night tucked them under a comforter on Mabel's back porch. Next morning, Mabel showed up in Gladys's kitchen. *Land sakes,* she said, *I thought I was too old for miracles.*

And she took it as a sign, promised to nurse her little foundlings from the river and find homes for them later.

Old Gladys's eyes twinkled as she told her story. *Miracle-worker,* she snorted. *You mark my words,* she said. *Things in this world ain't always what they appear t'be.*

THUNDER MOUNTAIN

About two thirds of the way up the mountain, just where the forest thins and the granite skullcap begins, and the view beyond is too spectacular for words, there is a large granite boulder, flat, about the size of the roof on an old Volkswagen bus.

In the beginnings, before the white man came and churned up the topsoil with his Jeeps and his ATVs, before silt washed down the mountain and filled in the crevices, you could stand on one end of that boulder, and your friend could stand on the other, and you could rock up and down, flexing your knees and raising and lowering your arms, Like two great cranes on a teeter-totter, and the mountain would respond with rumblings and thunderings from Deep Underground.

This was all explained by a certain Mr. Thunderbear. George Thunderbear, that was, of the Penobscot Nation.

"Bear," someone asked, (for that's what folks called him back then), "Generations of little Thunderbears, kids like your own, for hundreds of years must have played on that rock, bellied it back and forth and listened in awe to the thundering from the mountain. And they must have had a name for the rock, for the mountain itself. Something like *Thunder Mountain, doncha think?*"

Mr. Bear waited, as was his wont, to make sure his interlocutor was finished. Then, with a swallow and a licking of his lips, he said, "Yes. It was..." And he told the name. It had fourteen syllables, with just two vowels and forty-seven consonants, including exes, zees, seven diphthongs, x's, and clickings of the tongue. It cannot be recaptured here.

His listeners stepped back in awe. "But what does it mean?" they asked.

Again that smile and licking of lips – as if relishing his tale. "It means," he repeated, "it means White Man ask too many questions."

His listeners waited patiently for him to say more, but that was all he had to say.

SENSITIVITY TRAINING

Arnie Murphy was a huge man with a face to scare children — if it weren't for the kind eyes and the mirthful twist of his smile. Small town cop he was and fourth generation Mainer, with a family tree full of storytellers and pranksters.

But then came this new wave of young folks to town. "Homesteaders" they called themselves, settling in the hills and valleys "outback." Scary prospect they were for folks in town—stories abounded of cults and orgies and drugs for sale on the playgrounds.

But not for Arnie. No, not for Arnie. He'd gone to Sensitivity Training down in Portland to help him deal with this wave of newcomers. And there he sat at our kitchen table, telling story after story of the old days.

That little house just up the road? Why that used to be the schoolhouse, and he himself used to walk through our woods and right across our broccoli patch to get his learning from Ms. Betsy at the schoolhouse.

And that little church in the valley? Rumrunners used to store their hooch in the basement way back then. Big shoot-out with the Feds one winter night, and the rum got dumped through a hole in the ice right over there in the pond. Probably still there if anyone went to look for it.

And them? Arnie would turn away, shielding his eyes from the little marijuana seedlings sprouting in seed cups on the windowsill. *I don't even see them.* And he would continue with his stories. He was a small-town cop to be sure, but he was a fourth generation Mainer, and he'd been to sensitivity training down in Portland.

109

THE MAN WITH A GUN

The photograph is stark and powerful. Shot downwards from an old stone footbridge, it shows a magnificent white horse, trapped on his back between the boulders of a small brook. One leg is stretched awkwardly behind, hoof wedged between a log and a smaller rock. Terror gleams in the animal's eyes, and the stream is in turmoil from the thrashing head, the flailing hooves. The contrast between the soft white horse and the harsh, black boulders is extreme. In fact, the photograph might be black-and-white were it not for the vivid red splotches on the horses head, on the snow on the boulders in the brook.

What happened was this: It was wintertime, and a young woman, one of the newcomers to the county, attempted to ride the horse over the slippery stone bridge. At first, the animal balked. The woman insisted, and midway over the bridge, the horse stumbled and lost its footing. The young woman slipped off, unhurt. But the horse tumbled into the stream below. The woman raced to a nearby road to call for help.

That's when the photographer appeared at the bridge and began snapping pictures.

The young woman returned. The horse thrashed wildly in the stream below, heaving his head from side to side against the rocks. The snow around him was deep-red with blood. The young woman was terrified. She clambered down the rocks and braced herself against the horse's head, struggling to calm him, to control the thrashing. For almost half an hour, she remained there in the cold water, holding the horse's head, waiting for help to arrive.

Above her, a small crowd gathered on the bridge, and

the photographer continued to snap pictures.

With the arrival of the young woman's friends, the rescue began in earnest. Ropes were attached to the flailing feet. The horse was pushed, pulled, and twisted about. Then, after several hours of futile effort, one of the rescuers, a grizzled old-timer in the background, left and returned shortly with a gun. The crowd on the bridge gasped and jockeyed for position. The photographer took a picture of the gun.

By this time, the horse was exhausted; his head lay motionless in the young woman's lap. The man with the gun approached the rescuers, pointed to something in the stream. With that, the rescuers managed to free a trapped hind foot, and the horse begins thrashing again. The rescuers worked a small log under his shoulders, and, by lifting together, were able to elevate him slightly. The horse struggled violently, apparently sensing new hope. Then, in one supreme effort, he wrenched himself free and bolted up the bank of the stream. There, he stood, battered and bleeding, rocking unsteadily from side to side. The young woman went to him, talked soothingly, and led him out to the road. The horse faltered and stumbled but managed to keep his feet. The man with the gun followed the young woman to the road and talked with her, advised her on the care and treatment of her injured horse.

The following day, a local poet recorded the incident as some sort of triumph of spirit over dark matter. The horse was white, after all—though it was bloodied and missing one eye.

Saint Vincent at the Dump

At the transfer station this morning, Vinny, the keeper, grizzled and swarthy, glowering from his control booth. Not much gets past Vinny. Plastic bags in the recycling compactor? Nosiree, ma'am – not on Vinny's watch.

An elderly woman, bright-eyed, radiant smile, struggles at the compactor, manages, with help from a bystander, to dump a small avalanche of tin cans from a bag that says black-oil sunflower seeds. The compactor is overflowing, and the cans clatter on the floor.

Vinny appears, scowling, lumbering from his office. *Are those cat food tins?* he asks the woman. She appears nervous, even flustered.

Yes, she replies.

And how many cats do you have?

For such a bear of a man, his voice is remarkably soft and gentle.

Three, replies the woman. And she bends to pick up the cans from the floor.

The reason I ask, says Vinny, bending to help her with the cans... And he goes on to tell a lengthy story, sprinkled with profanities, about an elderly couple that once came past his window. Every fourth Friday they would come. Jesus Christ. Toting bags just like hers of cans scraped clean with the labels removed. *Pretty suspicious*, Vinny now says. So finally one day, he called – who was it? – some Agency on Aging, he believes it was. And a proper investigation was launched.

Come to find out, the old folks were eating the cat food themselves. By the fourth week of every month, their money would run out, and cat food, purchased in bulk by the boxful, was all they could afford.

Vinny pauses for effect. And that, he tells the woman at his compactor, is why he is worrying a little about her this morning.

The old woman just shakes her head and clucks her tongue.

And what ever become of them? she asks.

Last I heard, Vinny tells her, arrangements got made with local food kitchens. Meals on Wheels, programs like that.

The woman smiles happily. *Oh good,* she says, *I'm so glad. And you're so good to care,* she tells him. *But you don't have to worry about me,* she adds. *I really do have three cats. And everyone knows I've been a vegetarian all my life.*

Vinny pats her hand and turns to the bystander. *Them plastic bags you got there?* he growls. *Can't dump 'em here. That shit goes in the hole. Them batteries, too.*

And he points to a huge, gaping hole, gears grinding away at the bottom, just outside the door to his office.

The Game Warden
and the Griswold

Everyone loved Rusty Henderson, Regional Game Warden and raconteur extraordinaire. A *real* law enforcement officer he was with his shiny green uniform and big 35 millimeter gun at his hip. (Game biologists were a bit envious, he claimed. People took them for park rangers in their drab brown uniforms.)

And there Rusty sat, telling stories in my kitchen. I was interviewing him for a piece I was writing about a moose that had wandered into town. It was the biologists who did all the work, Warden Rusty admitted. They're the ones who anaesthetized him and carted him off into the forest. We just directed traffic and managed the crowd.

And Rusty went on to tell stories about dozens of other animal rescues and releases he'd been part of... But suddenly he stopped, staring at something behind me in my kitchen. *MY GOD* Rusty said, *Is that a Griswold?* He was pointing at a big, twelve inch cast iron frying pan hanging on the wall by the window.

I fetched the frying pan. Rusty shifted gears from moose rescues to Griswolds. *Best pans ever made.* Rusty said. His grandmother had nothing but. Twelve inchers especially rare. Collectors everywhere... Rusty's eyes shone. Eighty-five dollars he offered me for my Griswold.

I smiled and imagined him leaving my house, big thirty-five millimeter in one hand, frying pan in the other, packing iron as it might be. And I declined his offer. Whatever the pan had been worth to me yesterday, it was worth that tenfold today.

That night I dreamed of Rusty Hutchinson, crouched

over an open fire, moose steak sizzling in my big black twelve-inch Griswold frying pan.

NO PIG FOR SALE

We met in the yard of an old farmhouse. Sheds and outbuildings stood all around, and fields stretched off to woods in the background. "But that's absurd," I said to the weathered old farmer. I regretted it immediately; the old man's eyes narrowed and hardened in defense.

"Look, young feller," he said. "I'd like to help you out. You want to buy a pig; I got pigs. But, like I told you, there's only forty, fifty of 'em out there now."

I nodded. "And you can't spare any of them," I said, echoing, trying not to mimic, what I'd been told from the outset.

The old man ignored the sarcasm. "Nope, he said, can't spare any of 'em. Like I told you, I been getting that bread from the bakeries for near on sixty years now. First thing every morning, I take the truck up to Bangor and make the rounds. Now, I ask you, what am I going to do with all that bread if I got no pigs to eat it?"

What say? I squinted at the old man. Was he pulling my leg, testing me in some way?

The old man stood gazing out across his yard. "I've raised hogs all my life," he said. "Time was I had as many as four hundred of 'em out there. Now, people are wanting me to get rid of 'em. They say I'm too old. Why, I don't guess there's fifty hogs left out there now."

He turned to face me again. "Don't you see," he said, "the bread would rot without the hogs to eat it."

I nodded. A story was taking shape in my mind – the old man pitted against the urgings of family and friends, his ludicrous argument his last defense against their urgings. *What would I do with the bread?* It *was* ludicrous.

116

I fought the urge to smile. In fact, the old man was smiling a little himself, as if sharing a secret. "Sorry I can't help you," he said. "Come on over here; I'll show you my breadhouse."

The old man led the way across the yard, past a swing set and sandbox where small children were playing and glancing in our direction. Inside a small cabin, piles of bakery products – bread, doughnuts, pastries of all kinds – were heaped on the floor and crammed onto shelves. The smell of bread hung heavily in the air. In the far corner, a small wood-stove crackled; it was cozy in the cabin. A massive, overstuffed armchair squatted by the wood-stove, and the old man settled himself into it. He sat, for all the world, like a king in his throne room. Then he cleared his throat and began to talk. On and on he talked, his voice throaty and just above a whisper. He talked about the old days, the land he had once owned, about the war, about changes in the town, about animals he had raised and bargains he had struck. And he talked about his family, his wife Emmy, his children, his grand children and great grandchildren. His voice softened as he talked about the children, and there were tears in his eyes.

The old man got up to add a log to the fire and settled back in his chair. A light tapping came at the door. A child entered and climbed up on the old man's knee. "This is Jennifer," he said, obviously quite pleased with his visitor. From a shelf behind him, he took a package and handed it to the child. She left the cabin munching on a day-old strawberry tart.

The old man began talking again, now about the proper care of pigs – feed, breeding, ranging habits, pen sizes, and so on. Another little girl entered the cabin, and, shortly, she too ran out with a pastry in her hand.

The old man continued his monologue, drifting off into long digressions and reminiscences. I listened, fascinated, not so much by the stories, as by the steady stream of children that flowed in and out of the cabin. They came one-by-one. Each child settled on the old man's knee, suffered a proud introduction, and left with a happy smile and a bakery treat in hand. In the space of an hour, perhaps a dozen children came and went, never the same child twice.

In the end, I felt humbled by it all, even ashamed of myself a little. I had come to buy a pig, logically, practically, efficiently; I was prepared to dicker and negotiate. I left instead with a packet of jelly doughnuts under my arm – and the gentle reminder that there were ebbings and flowings at work in the universe that ran far deeper than my little hog-buying agenda. Here, at least, there was no pig for sale.

WILLIE KNOWS WHO DONE IT

The sirens and flashing lights seem strangely incongruous here, the sleek vehicles oddly misplaced. A rural dump, after all, lends itself more to mud-spattered trucks and garbage-packed sedans. The twisted figure on the stretcher, his grizzled face and thrift-shop clothing now officially shrouded, seems, even in death, to dig in his heels before gliding soundlessly into the gleaming, polished vault of the ambulance.

It is early morning. Seagulls swirl against a leaden sky. Gusts of wind, laden with grit and litter, blast across the landscape. Newspaper skitters like tumbleweed, skirts a row of fifty-gallon drums, and flattens against a ten-foot storm fence at the leeward perimeter. At the center of the dump, a soot-crusted shack, constructed of odds and ends of wood and sheet metal salvaged over the years, shudders and braces itself against the wind. Nearby, the emergency vehicles cluster like nervous thoroughbreds. Beyond, hulking piles of gravel and garbage await the bulldozer's blade.

A well-dressed young man, a reporter, it seems, wanders about snapping pictures and jotting in a notepad. He notices at last a figure standing against the storm fence, a tall, stoop-shouldered man, seemingly pinned there by the wind. Two policemen are with him. They turn away and walk quickly towards the shack. "Old man's crazy," one of them says. "Willie knows who done it, my ass. Willie's deader'n a doornail."

"Caleb ain't crazy," says the other. "He just don't want to talk to us."

"You figure he knows who done it?"

"No more'n Willie knows."

They pass from earshot. A seagull shrieks from the sky and perches atop a tangled pile of rope and broken stakes. The reporter observes it all, then crosses to the storm fence and stands next to the old man. "Your name Caleb?" he asks. The old man stares straight ahead, seemingly oblivious to his presence. Then, slowly, he turns his head. White whiskers cover his jaw; his eyes lurk deep in their sockets, red-veined and watery. He jerks his head towards the flashing lights.

"You with them?" he asks.

"No, not with them. Just want to hear your story."

"I didn't figure you was with them." He leans back against the fence, working his jaw and gazing across the dump. A small crowd has gathered at the outer end of the access road, held back by a single policeman. The old man eyes the reporter again. "How'd you get in here?"

"I got here early, just walked in. No one seemed to notice." The old man smiles, a quick, contemptuous smile, apparently not for the reporter.

"You a friend of Willie's?" asks the reporter.

The old man spits on the ground. "I been called worse," he says bitterly.

Across the dump, a siren wails briefly, and the emergency vehicles file out the access road, parting the crowd as they go. Behind, the lone policeman swings the heavy gate closed, sweeping the crowd back against a Dump Closed sign that runs the length of the gate.

The old man stands motionless, watching dispassionately as the crowd disperses, as a few curiosity-seekers squeeze through the gate and shuffle down the access road. A fine rain has begun to fall, but the old man does not move. He watches the curiosity-seekers, stiffening and clenching his jaw as they approach the shack and peer through the door, relaxing only when they turn away and disappear down the access road. Then, for long minutes, he leans back against the fence, gazing at the seagull-flecked clouds, letting the soft rain wash over his face. At last, he shudders and walks, limping a little, to the abandoned shack. The wind has abated with the coming of the rain, and his clothes hang damp and heavy. He disappears into the shack. The reporter hesitates, then follows. The old man appears to have forgotten him.

Inside, the shack reeks of oil and mildew. A solitary window, fly-specked and grimy, seems less to admit light than to siphon it off. Beneath the window, a tattered automobile seat squats on oil-soaked timbers. Crates and broken chairs line the walls. Just inside the door, the old man slouches in a peeling rocker. His hands lie limp in his lap, and he gazes absently out the window, past piles of garbage, to a mist-obscured horizon. The view has the appearance of an ancient, yellowed photograph. Nervously, across the doorway from the old man, the reporter perches on an empty crate.

It is silent inside the shack, silent except for the pinging of the rain on the roof and the muffled shrieking of the seagulls outside. At last, without shifting his gaze from the window, the old man breaks the silence. His voice is flat, gravelly, monotonous. "That's's Ben's seat you're in," he says.

The reporter starts to rise.

"But Ben ain't here today, so's you might as well stay put." He continues to gaze out the window, rocking almost imperceptibly back and forth.

Minutes pass. The old man shifts his gaze to his hands in his lap, then up into the rafters overhead. "Fella like you don't belong in a place like this," he exhales at last. There is nothing judgmental in his voice; he is just stating a fact. "Ain't nothin' here for you."

The reporter leans forward earnestly. "Will you tell me about Willie?"

The old man hangs his head against the back of his rocker. "Tell you about Willie?" he sighs.

There is a hint of mockery in his voice. "What you want t'know about Willie for?"

The reporter does not answer. The old man shivers and pulls his head forward. He glances at a small wood-stove in the far corner of the shack, then turns his gaze out the window again.

"Man like you couldn't understand about a man like Willie," he says wearily. "Long time ago, maybe..." The old man hesitates, rocking jerkily in his chair, then draws a deep breath and plunges on. "Back then, maybe you an' him coulda seed eye t'eye. Willie was gonna make somethin' of hisself back then, see? Had him this little place in town; his father give it to him, won it in a poker game. Willie was gonna have him a automobile repair shop there. He was good with his hands, real good. Fix most anything once he put his mind to it. Worked over t'the Sunoco station – leastways when he could..."

The old man pauses, a tense, pained look on his face; his hands clutch the arms of his rocker. "Headaches," he says hoarsely. "Willie had these headaches, see, faintin' spells sometimes. Fell off'n the barn roof when he was a kid. People like Willie – you gotta understand – he come from Outback. Old farm families; no cash; land all played

122

out. People in town called him a retard, wouldn't have nothin' to do with him. Willie's father done the doctorin' hisself. Lord knows, he done the best he could, but a fall like that, the kid needs a real doctor. Willie never did get over it, stutterin' and all, with his headaches and faintin' spells. And it didn't get no better neither. Fact, the older he got, the worser it got. Use t'sit under that window there. Sun'd come streamin' in, and Willie'd stretch out on his seat and try t'warm the hurt outa hisself."

The reporter leans forward, straining to hear. Throughout, the old man's voice has grown increasingly husky and faint. He is barely moving now, and his hands lie unmoving in his lap. A seagull shrieks overhead. For an instant, the old man's gaze flickers to the empty seat beneath the window; the muscles of his jaw tighten, and his fists clench in his lap.

"Wasn't much Willie wanted outa life," he says bitterly, "but he sure wanted that automobile repair shop. Figgered he could make something of hisself there all right. But he weren't about t'ask no favors neither. Nossir, he worked down t'the Sunoco sataion, pumpin gas, savin' hisself some startin-up money. Even after they took his place away from him, he didn't ask no favors. Zoned his place clean off the map, they did. Called it a eyesore – no foundation, no plumbing. Took it over for back taxes, the bastards. Run the dozer back and forth a couple times and built theirselves some new town offices. "

The old man shakes his head, spits into a can in the corner. "And still Willie didn't ask no favors. Went t'work for the railroad instead, layin' track, stayin' around wherever he could. Course, he couldn't keep it up. Nine, ten years, spells got so bad he had t'come back. The man needed help. Wasn't much the town could do about it neither – ceptin' maybe makin' him crawl in every week for his handout. After all, they was the ones that broke him. He knew that. They both knew that. Hated each other for it, too."

The old man is rocking jerkily, angrily, it seems. Now he lowers his eyes and gazes at his hands, large, gnarled from years of hard work. Gradually, the tempo of his rocking slows. He draws a deep breath and continues.

"Right about then, when it came time for the beggin', Willie stopped talkin' altogether. Never said another word. Course, some folks say he just didn't want t'talk, and some folks say it was just the old hurt finally takin' him down. Me, it seems t'me, you can't hold the two of them separate. Ten years layin' track, the hurtin' and the hatin' just simmering away til he couldn't get no words out past 'em. Time the railroad finished with him, the spunk was pretty much gone outa Willie. Couple, three years on the town dole, what with the beggin' and the achin' in his head, there weren't hardly no spunk left at all."

Now, for the first time, the old man looks directly at the reporter. "Maybe you can't understand that," he says accusingly, "beggin like that takin' the spunk outa a man." His eyes are hard, dry now. The reporter shifts in his seat, and the old man looks away, gazes out the window again, rocking gently, seeking his rhythm, flexing his fingers in his lap.

"I don't know how Willie come t'be in charge of the dump. Seven, eight years ago that was. Someone musta decided he had t'work for his handouts. One way or t'other, they set him up as the dump keeper, had him tendin' the fires, tellin' folks where t'dump their garbage and the like.

Those days, they still burned the garbage. That was before the 'vironmental people got on 'em. Fact, it weren't more'n a couple years after that they started buryin' the garbage. Sanitary landfill, they called it. Willie didn't like that none too well; he kinda liked tendin' the fires. But there wasn't nothin' he could do about it. An' course, time they got the landfill operation runnin' pretty good, then they started talkin' about transfer stations and the like – where they wouldn't need no dumpkeeper at all, just some engineer trained special for the job. Now, that was somethin' else, far as Willie was concerned, but I'm gettin' ahead a myself here...

"Like I said, time Willie come t'the dump, he was pretty beat. You could always tell when he was hurtin' – eyes all squinty an' shoulders all hunkered up. Folks in town musta figgered he'd just hunker himself into the fire one day an' be outa their hair for good. Well, tidn't work out that way."

The old man pauses here, stretching his legs out in front of him, massaging his knees with knobby fingers. There is an odd, little twist to his lips, almost a smile. "Nope," he says, setting his feet again and resuming his rocking, "tidn't work out that way at all. What happened was Willie started gettin' his spunk back. He never started talkin' again or nothin'; it was too late for that. But what y'gotta understand is that, after all those years, Willie finally had a place that was his'n. Course, it weren't really his'n; he knew that, and knowin' that didn't make him no fonder of the folks that set him up – 'specially with them bein' the same ones that had done him dirty in the first place. But it was somethin', somethin' he could set his teeth into, somethin' he could fight for. Once he got started, weren't nobody could take *that* away from him. Nossir, far as Willie was concerned, he was done with the crawlin' and beggin', and he was done with it for good. Course, be hard t'say what good it done him in the end. Real hard t'say."

The old man drifts away, lost in thought, rocking, gazing distantly out the window. When he speaks again, his visitor might have left in the interlude; it would not have mattered.

"Like I said, it weren't more'n a couple months after Willie come t'the dump here that he started gettin' his spunk back. First thing he done was t'build hisself this place. It don't look like much, but it sure looked like a lot t'Willie. Course, he weren't s'posed t'stay here nights, but he did most times anyhow. No one paid it no mind. Rest of the time, he'd stay with folks out back. They didn't like that none too well, what with him not talkin' an' all. But most times they'd take him in if he needed it bad enough. Course, a little later, when he'd got things turned his way some, they was always glad to see him. That was on account of the dump pickins."

Again, the old man pauses, ruminating, gathering his thoughts. "Dump pickins," he repeats. "That's what it all comes down to. See, when Willie first come t'the dump, folks used the place pretty much t'suit theirselves. Dumped stuff wherever they wanted t'dump it, picked up whatever they saw lyin' around they thought they might be needin'. Dump pickin'. Most everybody picked the dump. A few made a pretty good livin' off'n it, too, sellin' scrap metal an' the like. Course, if you broke it down, it was folks from town mostly throwin' the stuff out an' folks from outback pickin' it up. Folks like Willie, there wasn't much they couldn't find a use for. It was a way of life for 'em, not somethin' you'd expect 'em t'give up easy – not for the likes

126

of them in town, leastways. But, couple, three years after Willie took over the dump, that's what it come down to. Weren't Willie's fault neither. Course, he had his job t'do – no denyin' that. And by that time you might say he had no loyalties left one way or t'other. It was Willie he was lookin after, just hisself, and the more the pickins got regulated, the more pickins he got for hisself. That was part of the job; dumpkeeper got the pickins. But it weren't Willie that put up the signs; it was the town crew what come out and done that. Big signs, too, half a dozen of 'em, all along the access road. No dump pickin, they said. Fifty dollar fine for dump pickin. Course, no one knows why they ever wanted them signs in the first place. Wasn't no need for 'em. First night, they got shot up so bad you couldn't even read 'em. Police chief come out the next day and asked Willie if he knowed who done it. Told him t'nod his head when he said the right name. Willie just kept shakin' his head."

The old man chuckles to himself and rubs his knees. "Willie knowed who done it, all right. More'n that, he knew why they done it. But, like I said, he didn't have no loyalties left one way or t'other. Week or so later, the town crew come by again, puttin' up new signs. Only this time, the first sign was a big red one. 'No shootin' on the dump,' it said. Well sir, let me tell you, by the end of the week, them no pickin' signs was shot up pretty bad, but that no shootin' sign weren't no more'n a pole standin' there along side a the road. See, some folks don't like bein' told what t'do. Boss'n theirselves is a way a life with 'em, and it don't change easy. Course, the shootin' never was a real issue – just a way of expressin' theirselves. Bye'n by, it pretty much petered out – leastways for the time bein'. But the pickin' now, that was somethin' else. There was them that wasns't about t'give up their dump-pickin right for nobody. And that's where Willie come into the picture. Got his nose broke more'n once for it, too. Course, it was his job t'enforce the rules, but that ain't why he done it. He done it t'get the pickins for hisself. Sell 'em off, he would. Cheap. But just enough t'get him a little spendin' money. That's why the folks outback started gettin' glad t'see him. Started chargin' him for stuff and borrowin' money off'n him. Some folks. Most of 'em wasn't too happy about the situation – havin' it against the law t'pick the dump, havin' Willie expectin' 'em t'pay him for stuff they'd always got for free. 'Specially 'cause it was Willie."

The old man stops his rocking altogether now, and stares at his hands, watching them move in his lap. "So, y'see," he says softly, "with the town on one side, tellin' him t'enforce the rules, and the outback folks on t'other side, thinkin' the rules was some kinda communist plot, Willie had got hisself between a rock and a hard place. A real hard place. And that was only the beginnin', too. Things got worse after that. Had t'get worse; weren't no place else they could go."

Again, the old man falls silent. When he resumes, he is gazing out the window again, rocking nervously back and forth. His fingers twitch in his lap, and his voice catches in his throat. "Like I said, couple times Willie got hisself beat up pretty bad. Happened nighttimes mostly. Folks wasn't s'posed t'use the dump nights. Sign out front said, No dumpin' on Sundays or after sundown. That was t'give the fires a chance t'burn down. But you couldn't hardly read that sign. It'd been there longer'n anyone could remember. No one ever paid it no attention, neither – just like no one paid the dump pickin' signs no attention.

"Funny the town never did replace that old sign. What they done instead was to put up the gate. That was three, maybe four, years ago, just before they changed over from burnin' t'landfill. Willie was s'posed t'close the gate on Sundays and at sundown. Thursdays, too, come t'think on it. Big, heavy gate. Iron posts set in concrete. Weren't much anyone could do about that gate. It stopped the night pickin' – most of it leastways. But it didn't stop 'em from dumpin' their garbage. Right up against the gate they'd throw it. Guess they figgered they wasn't responsible for rememberin' dumpin' schedules and the like. They'd druv in four maybe five miles, and no dang fool sittin at a desk in town was gonna tell 'em t'turn around and haul it back home again. Nossir, they'd dump it right there at the gate. Still do, some of 'em. Course, it was Willie's job t'clean it all up. Wasn't nobody else around t'do it. Most time, he knew who made the mess too. Laid in wait for' em one time. No tellin' what he figgered t'do. For all anyone knows, he was gonna open the gate, let 'em come in and dump their garbage. One way or t'other, they beat him up real bad that time. Put him in the hospital for near a week – first time he'd ever been there. When he come back, somebody'd writ filth on the walls here and dumped a bucket a excrement all over the floor."

The old man snorts disgustedly. Throughout, he has grown increasingly agitated. Now, he sighs deeply and rests his head against the back of his chair. Slower and slower he rocks, gazing out the window through half-shut eyes. When he speaks again, his voice is barely audible, low and hoarse. "Funny thing about Willie... All that trouble he got tryin' t'run the dump – that didn't seem t'bother him none. Even the beatin' up he'd bounce right back from.

Course, it weren't always easy t'tell what Willie liked and didn't like, what with him not talkin' and all, but, often as not, you could read it on his face. Like when he come back from the hospital and seen the excrement all over his place, why, he just buckled down and cleaned it all up. That kinda shit didn't bother him none. It was the other kind – like when he heard about them changin' the dump from a burnin' dump to a landfill operation. His face just screwed up tight like he was havin' one of his headaches. Same thing with the signs and the new gate. It didn't matter much t'Willie one way or t'other *what* got done – only *how* it got done, how it all went on behind his back with him like some fish in the rain barrel. Six, seven years of it by that time. Seemed like every day the folks in town was comin' up with new regulations and the like, takin' over *his* dump, runnin' it like a post office or a hospital or somethin'. Willie saw what was happenin'. He saw the writin' on the wall long before them engineer fellers come by talkin' about transfer stations and the like. And the writin' he saw weren't just a bunch of dirty words neither."

For long minutes now, the old man is silent, rocking almost imperceptibly back and forth, back and forth. Outside, the rain is falling harder; the reporter crouches at the edge of his seat, straining to hear over the pounding on the roof. At last, the old man continues. "Yessir, Willie saw the writin' on the wall all right. An' the more writin' he saw, fancy writin', writ by fancy folks in town, the more he sunk his teeth into takin' care a business out here. I ain't sayin' he started no trouble, but he sure's hell didn't do nothin' t'stay out of it neither. Started carryin' a hunk a iron pipe around with him, for one thing. Most folks understood that pretty good. Them that didn't done what they always done

130

– fixed Willie so's he wouldn't bother 'em none. I'd come in here some mornins, and it's be noon b'fore I got him back on his feet. Whatever it was gettin' into Willie, makin him fight meaner, same thing was gettin' into them dump-pickin' fellers. They knew what was happenin' same's Willie did. More'n more cruisers out here patrollin'. More'n more fancy new bulldozin' equipment. They knew things was changin', an they didn't like it no better'n Willie did. Fact, the dump pickin' weren't even a issue no more. Time them engineer fellers first started comin' around, three, four months ago, only thing left was the hatefulness – folks shootin' and raisin' hell jist outa spite..."

Again, the old man pauses. He continues to sit with his eyes half-shut, barely rocking, gathering his strength. At last, he pulls his head forward and opens his eyes wide. He is shivering slightly in his damp clothes. He glances at the small wood-stove in the back corner of the shack, then rests his head against the back of his chair and stares out the window again. When he speaks, his voice is a broken whisper. "Funny thing," he rasps, "Willie caught in the middle like that, both sides closin' in on him like some kinda garbage compactor. An' him bein the garbage. Real bad headaches he was gettin' then, blackin' out more'n more. And, like I said, it wasn't the beatin-ups that was doin' it neither; it was them engineer fellers out there, surveyin', poundin' stakes. Committees from town, too, fancy folks comin' out, talkin' about recyclin' plants and the like. Willie'd stay away from 'em, sit in here, just kinda holdin' his head in his hands. Hard thing t'watch a man sufferin' like that. Real hard. Two, three days he'd be down sometimes. But danged if he wouldn't bounce right back. Nossir, Willie never give up. Right t'the end, he never give up. Folks in town, more'n more they saw thet was gonna have t'deal with him. Like the clock was turned back all them years – only they couldn't just zone his place off'n the map no more. Nossir, things was different this time: Willie'd learned how things worked over the years, and there wasn't nothin' else he could do 'cept keep on fightin'. Same with them dump-pickin fellers. I don't guess they hated Willie no more'n he hated them, way down rock bottom. It was like they had t'get somethin' outa their system, an' they just kept bumpin' into each other. Most every night, they was trouble then, fightin' meaner'n meaner. More'n a few mornings, I come across Willie out there beat pretty near t'death. Shootin' too. I guess they spent better'n half their time over there t'the town garage diggin' lead outa the bulldozing equipment. Mornins them engineer fellers'd come by, and their stakes an' strings an' little flags'd be all over the place. Police come questionin' Willie about it, askin' if he knew who done it. Willie just kept shakin' his head. He knew who done it, all right. Fact, some folks'll tell you he done it himself. Man tells you that, he's a liar. But it don't matter none now, and it didn't matter none then. One way or t'other, police started patrollin' out here regular. That quieted things down some, but it didn't do nothin' for the hatefulness. That just simmered there, smoldered away like them old dump fires use't do back in the old burnin' days – just smolderin' away, waitin' for some windy night when everyone'd turned his back, thinkin' everything was under control...."

The old man stops suddenly and jerks his head forward. "Course, there weren't no *point* to it," he says angrily. "Change comin' on like that, like the frost comin' into the ground, ain't nothin *nobody* can do to stop it. Mark my words, day won't be gone before them engineer fellers are out there again, measurin' and calculatin' and poundin' their goddam stakes." He clutches his elbows and doubles over in his chair, shivering violently.

The reporter watches for a minute, waits for the old man to straighten up and resume his rocking. Then he moves across the room and crouches at the wood-stove in the corner. The door is slightly ajar; inside, a fire is already laid. Behind him, the old man draws a deep, raspy breath. "Musta happened just about then," he says dispassionately. "Willie never laid it up ahead a time." The reporter pulls a red butane lighter from his pocket and shoots a six-inch jet of flame into the tinder. Then he rises and stands by the stove, toying with the lighter and watching the old man. At last, he jerks his head towards the door.

"What did you tell them out there?" he asks.

At first the old man is silent, ignoring him. Then he spits on the floor. "Asked 'em why the cruiser weren't out by the gate last night." He spits again. "Told 'em leastways Willie might a got hisself some help if the cruiser was there."

"Do you know what happened?"

"Willie blacked out for good is what happened."

"I mean...."

"You mean bullshit!" He wipes spittle from his chin with the back of his hand. "I been sittin' here half the mornin' tellin' you what happened. Like I said, it's hard, real hard, for a feller like you t'understand." The old man tapers off. He sighs deeply and slumps in his chair, weary, resigned, gazing out the window again, a pinched, pained look on his face. The reporter watches him closely. "You the man who took care of Willie when he fell off the roof?" he asks abruptly.

The old man continues to gaze out the window, working his jaw slowly. "Did the best I could," he says softly. Then, as the reporter moves to the door, he asks, "You workin' for the newspapers?"

The reporter turns in the doorway. "Yes."

"You gonna print all this up?"

"No."

Now the old man looks at the reporter, searchingly, confused at last.

"Like you said, it's real hard for a feller like me to understand."

The old man nods his head and sinks deeper into his chair. The reporter leaves him there, rocking gently, gazing wearily through half-shut eyes.

Outside, it is raining hard. Men in Day-Glo slickers are peering through transits, pounding stakes, calling back and forth in voices muffled by the rain. The reporter steps around their stakes, walks slowly down the access road, and squeezes through the gate. Already, trash has begun to accumulate against the Dump Closed sign – shiny plastic bags, hurled from car trunks, bulging and glistening in the rain; loose trash, kicked from truck beds; brown paper bags, dark with rain, burst at the seams, spilling their sodden innards. The reporter shakes his head in disgust and walks quickly to a red sports car parked just up the road. The engine roars to life. In the rearview mirror, the dump vanishes behind a curtain of rain.

WILDERNESS RESCUE:
A TRUE STORY

Mid-afternoon on July 26, 2011, a warm but overcast day. Three kids and I were working deep in the woods at The Great Pond Mountain Conservation Trust in Orland, Maine. Half an hour earlier, at the campus of KidsPeace New England in Ellsworth, we'd loaded up an eight-seater van with loppers, clippers, and bowsaws for volunteer work at what's popularly known as The Wildlands. The work was part of an outreach program for troubled youth, and, as coordinator of the program, I often brought kids to this wild and beautiful place, where they had an opportunity to connect with the natural world, contribute to the community – and have lots of fun, to boot.

On this particular day, on the drive over from Ellsworth, we'd received a call from Cheri Domina, Executive Director of the Trust, to the effect that a moose was loose in downtown Bucksport, just a few miles away. Plans called for releasing the moose in the Wildlands; she promised to keep us posted. Now, the kids worked hard, opening up a trail to the new Baker Brook camping area, eagerly anticipating a second call from Cheri Domina.

Eight miles away over in Bucksport, Denise Gordon looked out her kitchen window, and the glass of water she was holding shook in her hand. Moose have that effect on people, and the current moose, standing not twenty feet away with one foot in her marigolds was no different. Gordon reached for her camera, but it wasn't where she'd left it, and the moose was already "meandering" away. Gordon rushed outside and jumped in her car. Inexplicably, she had her camera now and managed to snap several pictures as the moose ambled down Bayview Avenue towards Dunkin' Donuts and the Hannaford Supermarket parking lot.

That same day, an hour or so earlier, Bucksport Police Officers Ernie Fitch and Steve Bishop were handling routine police business when the first of many calls came in. Moose sighted. Young moose at Bayview Drive. Traveling down Route #1. Dunkin' Donuts parking lot. Heading towards the river into heavy tourist traffic. Together, with Chief Sean Geagan, Fitch and Bishop rushed to the scene. They were joined shortly by Bucksport Police Sergeant David Winchester and by numerous members of the Bucksport Fire Department. What followed, by all later accounts, was a masterpiece of crowd control, inter-agency cooperation, and wildlife management.

Game Warden Mark Hutcheson of the Maine Department of Inland Fisheries and Wildlife (MDIFW) was on his day off, heading east from Ellsworth, when he received a call from his long-time friend Steve Bishop. "We got a moose in town!" Hutcheson relayed Bishop's call to the Greenville Office of the Maine Department of Inland Fisheries and Wildlife. He then drove quickly to his home, changed into uniform, and headed for Bucksport in a truck with all the insignia and flashing lights of the Maine Warden Service.

As he drove, Hutcheson had a funny feeling about this particular moose. It was probably the same one he'd run into two days earlier, a young moose, backing up traffic on the Downeast Highway just east of Toddy Pond. As cameras clicked, Hutcheson had managed to herd the moose off the road and back into the woods. "Four different times he pinned his ears back and came right at me. The ears are the barometer of how he feels. If the ears are forward, he's attentive and listening to you. But if he's mad, they're going to be pinned back flat against his head." Now, two days later, Hutcheson was about to meet his young friend again.

Meanwhile in Bangor, at the offices of MDIF's Wildlife Division (not to be confused with the Warden Service), Game Biologists Lee Kantar (moose specialist), Brad Allen (bird specialist), and Randy Cross (bear specialist) were going about their business when the call came in from regional headquarters in Greenville. On this particular day, Allen was not in uniform, but opted to join Biologists Cross and Kantar. "I'm a bird guy," Allen said, "and Lee comes down the hall and says we've got a moose that needs to be tranquilized in Bucksport. And I asserted myself only because I was available, and I live in Bucksport, and I know the cops down there and the wardens, and so I kind of went along just for the ride, and I stood in the background and tried to be useful. I served as staff photographer more than anything else."

Back in Bucksport, the moose continued his journey past Dunkin' Donuts and towards the downtown area. While others stopped traffic and kept the crowds back, Mark Hutcheson, joined now by Warden Brian Tripp, also of the MDIFW, worked closely with Bucksport Police Officers to calm and contain the moose. Traffic was heavy, the Hannaford Supermarket parking lot was full of onlookers as was the cemetery up the hill across the street.

"We were concerned about the traffic light area," recalled Winchester, "the Hannaford shopping area, just because of the time of the day, the time of year. So we were concerned about that and we were just trying to flood the area with officers to push the moose back out of that area.

So the fire department responded as well and they had as many as ten members who came along for traffic control and pedestrian control. Everyone wanted to see it - including us... "

At one point, according to Hutcheson, the moose circled around the supermarket and came out where a "bunch of kids on a bicycle tour" were having lunch. Hutcheson, who had spent much of his early life working ranches and guiding elk and mule deer hunts in Colorado, came running, shouting, extending his arms, making himself appear as large as possible. The bicycle tour kids "scattered like butterflies," according to Hutcheson, and the moose veered away towards a fenced in backyard adjacent to the Hannaford parking lot. "There's no way to drive a moose," said Hutcheson. "He's like a buffalo. You can only drive a moose where he wants to go."

For all of that, wardens and officers, working together were able to get the moose into the fenced-in yard adjacent to the parking lot. The fence was low and flimsy, but they surrounded the yard and managed to keep the moose from jumping out. By all accounts, the moose was calm, just circling the yard, waiting for Lee Kantar and his team of Wildlife Biologists to arrive.

There were two major concerns at this point. Safety of the crowd was paramount. There were perhaps thirty people in the Buck Memorial Cemetery across the street and a larger, swelling number in the Hannaford parking lot. Tourist traffic was particularly heavy, and, according to Sergeant Winchester, "Everyone wanted to stop because they saw Game wardens, law enforcement. At one point, I was carrying a shotgun, just because we didn't know what might happen. So everyone wanted to stop and see... We had people holding infants, trying to get closer. Well, it's a wild animal; it's a big animal. Lucky for us we had skilled people controlling the situation."

The second major concern was safety of the animal. Still a few miles away, Kantar, Cross, and Allen prepared themselves for the encounter. As Kantar put it, "I mean, we're driving down in the truck, zipping down to Bucksport as fast as we can, and we're thinking about, I mean, what are the things we're thinking about? Can we even immobilize this animal? Is he healthy? What's the temperature? How's he reacting to the heat? We were on the phone to Cheri Domina, talking about where to release it, and we hadn't even gotten there yet. Then, when we do get there," Kantar continued, "when we arrive at a scene, we have to make a visual judgment on the condition of the animal, – whether it has to be euthanized or whether its in good enough shape to survive the stress of anesthesia and release. We also have the whole public safety issue: is it feasible to remove that animal safely? Ideally, when we show up at a scene, there's not a crowd of people standing around with cameras. This all takes a lot of coordination..."

"Sometimes stress, even from heat is enough to put them over the edge," added Allen. "In this case, when we arrived, the animal was in a fenced in area and was just chilling out. Nobody was screaming and the crowd was well under control. Fortunately, it was an overcast day, and we were able to keep him cool."

Inside the Hannaford Supermarket, Kyle Pomeroy was working in the meat room when he heard people talking about a moose outside the store. Pomeroy had seen "lots of moose" in the course of his young life, but it was always "cool" to see one. He punched out for his lunch break and joined the crowd outside. According to Pomeroy's account, the moose was corralled in the backyard of a nearby house, and police were keeping the onlookers well back across the parking lot. They were concerned that the sound of cars starting would startle the moose, so no one was allowed to leave. Shoppers and "lots and lots" of tourists waited patiently for biologists to arrive and tranquilize the moose." Pomeroy who had grown up in Maine hunting with his father, seemed to know a lot about moose. He guessed that the young moose had been "kicked out of his territory by a more mature bull and was looking for his own territory." Now he watched from across the parking lot as a man in a tan uniform slipped through the crowd and approached the moose. Pomeroy did not know that he was watching Lee Kantar, the man to whom the moose would soon owe his life.

"Chemical immobilization," according to Kantar, is exactly what it sounds like, and it's come a long way from its early days half a century ago when animals would "be incapacitated but would still experience shock and pain trauma." On this particular day, Kantar prepared a mixture of Xylazine and highly regulated Ketamine, a mixture widely used by veterinarians for tranquilizing large animals. All Wildlife Biologists receive training in dosages and procedures every three years, and they operate under the auspices of a trained veterinarian. There's what they call a "high therapeutic index," which allows them to be less than exact in the dosage. Kantar himself, specializes in moose; Cross has immobilized thousands of bears. "All of us," Kantar added, "have some level of capture and immobilization experience."

In the current situation, Kantar and Cross did not have

their pole syringe or "jabstick" with them, and it quickly became clear that a hand-held syringe would not work; an extension was needed. So they came up with a "modified jabstick," according to Mark Hutcheson. "We took a head snare used to snag coons or porcupines or whatever. And I took some green duct tape I had in my truck and was able to tape on the syringe. And there we had it – an improvised jabstick, almost six feet long."

Now came a critical time in the proceedings. "Even in a perfect world, Kantar said afterwards, "when you drug an animal, it takes ten minutes or more for that animal to fall asleep." And those ten minutes can seem like hours, because there's so much that might go wrong. The moose in this case might stagger down to the river and drown. He might freak out altogether and stampede through the crowd. He might succumb to heat exhaustion, or he might rush into traffic and cause an accident. "At the same time," Kantar pointed out, "We're not veterinarians. We are trained, and we try to do quasi-care. It's a basic principle of chemical immobilization that, whoever immobilizes that animal is then responsible for the welfare of that animal, the treatment of that animal. And so that's everything from the basic ABC's—breathing, circulation and all that—to caring for any wounds, whatever, until that animal is reversed and sent off into the woods. At the same time, that doesn't mean we're going to cradle it in our arms like a baby. But we're going to do our best to keep the animal in good shape..."

Every effort was made to keep the moose calm and "in good shape." The police had stopped all traffic; the crowd was held back and encouraged to stay quiet. "I literally had my hands over his eyes while we had him down,"

Hutcheson recounted. "Then we found a bandana." Tripp crouched nearby, calming the animal. Someone removed her socks, and Randy Cross stuffed them in the moose's ears. "They'll react to sound quicker than anything when they're sedated," according to Hutcheson. "If you can keep his eyes covered and you don't have the stimulation of the sounds..."

As Brad Allen put it later, "I think one thing you should appreciate is how much care everybody was giving the animal. I mean, we're sitting there poking needles into this thing. Randy's on his brisket so he can breathe; we've got his eyes protected with a cloth, so we don't get twigs and sticks in them and startle him more. I mean this moose, as Lee says, if we can anthropomorphize him, is saying in his head, 'This really sucks. I've got four people I'm not really fond of manhandling me...' I mean, he's frightened."

Today, Winchester has nothing but praise for the police, the firemen, the wardens, and the biologists, all working together. He emphasizes the fact that, if it weren't for Lee Kantar, his expertise, it would have been necessary to euthanize the moose. Instead, "They put together a plan to tranquilize it. Once hit with the needle the moose got lethargic and sleepy and just fell over. The team loaded him onto that orange tarp and into the back of a truck. They took him four or five miles away into Orland to be released."

Great Pond Mountain Conservation Trust, Orland, Maine. Director of the Trust Cheri Domina: "I was driving home from Ellsworth that afternoon when I got a call on my cell phone from Lee Kantar, who said they were approaching Bucksport about to capture a young moose, and could they release it in the Wildlands. I said sure, and

142

asked for a call back when transport was imminent. I called the folks who were working with the KidsPeace group in the Wildlands, to give them a heads up, and went home to see if my visiting parents and my kids wanted to see a moose released. It was a treat to see this moose, and to watch the wardens and biologists doing their job..." Domina kept her cell phone handy as she awaited the call about the moose's imminent transport.

Back in the Wildlands, the KidsPeace work crew was halfway down the Campground Trail when the second call came in from Domina. Biologists and game wardens had successfully sedated the moose and were transporting it by truck to the forest where the boys, Scott, Arjuna, Jay, and Mikey were hauling and piling brush. When the moose call came in, their eyes lit up. Adolescents themselves, with sufficient trauma in their own lives, they seemed to identify with this fourteen-month-old moose.

So, they quickly packed up their tools, hopped in the van, and went to intercept the truck.

There were three biologists present, one not in uniform, two game wardens, and a moose in the back of the truck. The four boys and their chaperones followed the truck to a clearing in the forest. There, the boys helped pull the moose, wrapped in an orange tarp, from the back of the truck. They watched as moose biologists, led by Kantar, administered a shot in the ear, an antidote (Yohimbine) to the tranquilizer. At the same time, the wardens attached bright blue identification tags to the moose's ears.

After about half an hour, the moose began to move. A significant crowd had assembled near the boys. "This moose will need a name," called out Mark Hutcheson. "How old are you?" he asked Jay. "Fourteen," Jay answered.

"What's your name?" Hutcheson asked. Arjuna and Scott and Mikey looked at Jay in awe. Jay responded, and Hutcheson officially named the moose in Jay's honor.

All photographs of the event show Jay the boy beaming from ear to ear. It was in that smile that I first saw the twining of two stories – a troubled boy, a troubled moose, both trying to make their way in a world not intended to be alien, but alien nevertheless. That night, it can be hoped, the boy slept well, dreaming that a moose carrying his name roamed the forest, free and safe, protected by good men in official uniforms.

In fact, at this point, for all of Jay's wishes, survival of the moose was anything but a sure thing. According to Kantar, "The capture and release of any wild animal is always problematic. Because... is it worth it? We all want to believe that we can save the captured animal and drop it off some place, and it's a happy ending. But the reality of a wild animal is that it's up against a lot of things, and there is trauma to an animal that gets moved by a bunch of people. You know, one of the things that I always get a chuckle out of is when you hold a wild animal, everyone wants to pet it. But it's not a domestic dog. Its sense of having a person next to it, the scent of a person, the touch of a person, is not a pleasant thing at all..."

"There's a human tendency to anthropomorphize everything," said Allen.

"And you're probably going to do a lot more of it in your story," added Kantar.

Allen and Kantar went on to describe other dangers to a young moose. This would be the moose's first winter on his own, and, as Allen put it, "He won't have mom as a snowplow." Kantar added, "Then, there's a whole host of parasites." For moose of all ages, there's always brainworm, but for calves especially, there are other worms and also something called the winter tick that can weaken them and make them vulnerable in the springtime. As for predators, a human being in his automobile is the most dangerous, but there's always the black bear to be concerned about. "Mom is very good at protecting that cub from bears," Allen said, "but this little guy's on his own now. Ever see a skull of a black bear? That's not designed to eat blackberries."

Back in the clearing in the Wildlands, Jay the boy watched as his namesake, with considerable hoisting from his rescuers, struggled to his feet, peed for what seemed like long minutes, and moved haltingly towards the forest. Would he have family and friends to support him? Probably not; he'd been on his own all summer, and, as Brad put it, "Lee mentioned the first year being difficult. But how about the first summer of the moose being on his own away from his mom? Might that have led to some of his curious behavior?"

Kantar added, "Yeah, and that's a good point. Because in May, when the majority of moose are calving, mom's previous calf or calves are with her and they would be driven off. And of course, when they're driven off, they're going to be off on their own, wandering around out of mom's jurisdiction, and they're going to get into trouble."

But how about growing up, reproducing, having a family of his own? "Well," Lee explained, "he's able to reproduce already. But he's got to compete with the big bulls. And there's the rub – literally. He may be able to reproduce, but he's not going to have a lot of opportunities. He's only about five hundred pounds now. As he matures, he'll be more competitive."

By this point in the story, the young moose was still in sight, moving slowly into the shadows at the far end of the clearing. Twice he looked back at his rescuers, at the small crowd of onlookers. He seemed small and vulnerable, but wardens and biologists assured the onlookers that he would be okay; he seemed "comfortable" in his new home.

Three days later, Anna Bigelow awoke early in her cabin on French's Island in Alamoosook Lake. Something was happening outside. It was midday, she said, and he swam over from the Great Pond Mountain. side of the lake, strolled around the east side of the island and then went up onto Baker's Island to the south. He came back towards the west side of our place, but the dogs barked and he swam away. I have a short video I took..." (Video available upon request)

As Mark Hutcheson later put it, this would have been natural behavior for a moose – to hang around a lake, especially a lake, adjacent as Alamoosook is, to the Wildlands where the moose had been released. It would also be natural for the moose to follow the watercourse wherever it might lead – in this case back into the town of Orland, then Bucksport.

Wednesday, August 3, 2011. 9:32 AM. Once again calls came in to the BPD. Sergeant Winchester was at home when he received a call from Officer Dan Harlan. "He's back!" Winchester made it clear that, while public safety was paramount, once again, every effort should be made to save the young moose.

This time, the moose did not come into town. Instead, he made his way north through the woods parallel to Nicholson Avenue. "We monitored him as best we could," said Winchester, "and I got a call a short time later that he was up by the Health Center (Bucksport Regional Health Center). And it just happened to be that particular day that we had a warden in the area. So we lucked out. And then we lucked out again, because the Health Center has construction going on and they had a bunch of fencing that was connected, so they were able to push the moose towards this fenced area, and when it walked inside, they just gated it. So once again, the moose is in a fenced area. And again we just stood by and waited for the biologists."

"We were half expecting this," said Lee Kantar from his office in Bangor. This time, the call came in from Warden Brian Tripp. Tripp had been instrumental in the first capture and release, but this time, "The second capture was all Brian Tripp," according to Allen. "Brian got him into that enclosure, and all we did was walk down there and immobilize him." I told Brian, "I want you involved in every wildlife capture, because when we show up, they're already behind fences."

This time around, Kantar and Cross and Allen, joined by John Depue and Lisa Bates, had their official "jabstick" with them. Once again, the crowd was an issue; this was a congested area with the Health Center, schools, ballfields, and an apartment complex; someone even tried to feed him ice cream. Still, as Allen later put it, "The scene was totally set for us. The police did a great job. The crowd was held well back, and the moose was calm."

And, as before, every effort was made to keep the moose calm and safe. Once again, a bandanna was wrapped over his eyes and socks were stuffed in his ears, and once again, he was eased onto the big orange tarp, and loaded into the back of a truck. But this time, he wasn't taken to the Wildlands. "We drove a good hour out of Bucksport," said Allen, "beyond Bangor, north of the Stud Mill Road." And there, this moose named Jay began the next chapter of his life. He'll be hard to miss with his bright blue ear ornaments.

But the story does not necessarily end there, does not necessarily have a happy ending. As Kantar explained, "I mean, he might get shot or be hit by a car. Or be found dead from some disease. Also, we've rescued this animal twice; can we afford to do it again?" Lee paused. "But this is a very good story, with a very happy ending so far."

And, at this point in the story, the two Jays went their separate ways. As Allen said of the moose, "He was an adolescent animal that made some decisions that got him in trouble. Fortunately, we had the resources to bail him out. Next time we might not be there to help him. Hopefully there won't be a next time. I hope, for his sake, we never see him again."

Postscript: There is a widely circulated photograph of Biologists Lee Kantar and Randy Cross, along with Wardens Mark Hutcheson and Brian Tripp, posing in a portrait with the young moose in this story. Biologist Brad Allen wonders, "What are those four idiots doing standing next to a perfectly healthy moose?" It is critical for the public to understand that the animal in the picture is heavily sedated, just recovering from chemical immobilization. Under normal circumstances, no one should EVER approach a wild animal. The animal is not cute, and it is not a household pet.

ALL THE LOST CHILDREN

Author's Note: The following four sketches are lifted from a larger collection of writings about children, "children in crisis" they are called, housed in residential treatment centers around the northeast. My own experience with these kids involved a forest reclamation project through something called The Great Pond Mountain Conservation Trust in Orland, Maine.

BIG BRENDA

Oh such a big girl she was, this Brenda, beefy, with a bearish gait as she lumbered through the forest. The other kids trailed behind her, these lost and troubled children, teenagers all, wards of the state, conduct disordered in some cases, or lost in worlds of their own.

They were on a community service project this day. Staff tagged along with them, but Brenda was their leader. Other kids were smaller, smarter, quicker, and cleverer by far. The brightest among them, not to mention staff involved, wondered what it would be like to be Brenda, to be so big, so ungainly, so unpretty. Rumor had it that she'd thrown some bully through a window at her school back home, conduct disordered as she was.

Another time, she'd refused to follow an order from a teacher she considered rude and disrespectful. The teacher had approached her, gotten in her face; she'd hunkered up her shoulders and balled up her fists. The police had been called, and it was shortly after that that she was placed in *residential treatment*, as it was called. She did well there; which was why she was eligible for this community service project and and found herself trekking through the woods, smaller kids and staff trailing along behind her.

And it was just then that little Mikey, quick as a goat, bolted ahead, slipped on a mossy rock, and lay screaming in the leaves, his leg fractured just above the ankle.

And it was Brenda who bent over him, wrapped his leg tightly in her jacket, lifted him in her arms, and carried him sure-footedly half a mile back to the unmarked van in the parking lot.

The other kids tagged along behind. As did staff members present. Brenda was their leader, after all; there was no question about that.

EMMA – HER SECRET PLACE

Thirteen years old she is, a sweet girl by any measure, full Maliseet by birth, with high cheekbones, deep-set eyes, and dark hair braided to her shoulders. Beautiful she is. And troubled. She has suffered too much for a child so young. Fetal syndromes, childhood beatings, death, alcohol, always chaos in the family.

Now she lives with other children, children like herself, Children in Crisis, they are called. Today, she is off in the forest, part of an Outreach Project. (Community Service, it is called, working to clear the puckerbrush from a hilltop, creating a viewshed, they call it, where visitors can gaze upon the mountains in the distance.)

But Emma has disappeared, gone off from the group. Sounds of pruning and sawing come from behind a large boulder just down the hillside.

Respectfully (for Emma has long since earned the respect of all who know her), the group continues with its work, until it is time to pack up for the day.

Then they find Emma – in a leafy bower she has created, sitting cross-legged on the pine needles, a little smile on her lips, gazing out to the mountains in the distance.

NOT THE BOSS OF ME

What a stubby boy he was! Came about up to my armpit. But solid. Oh god was he solid. And strong as an ox. Stubborn too. He had to be stubborn; that was the only tool he had. Beaten and abused all his life, thirteen years old, dull as dishwater, no social skills or wit about him, stubborn was his secret power. Told to go clean his room or whatever, he would glare stupidly, roll his shoulders up around his ears, and bellow, *YOU'RE NOT THE BOSS OF ME.*

Anyone who ever worked with Chuckie will remember that sound - like some howling from deep in a cave. I was working with Chuckie at the time, Childcare Work it was called, and Chuckie was one of my charges. I learned to handle him in a way, to not back him into a corner, to give him plenty of space to make up his own mind about things. I drove him "home" one time, for a few days of respite (it was called) with his people - an uncle, drunk on the doorstep when we got there, a dilapidated mobile home with high-pitched voices from inside, and three mangy dogs roaming about, pissing on junk cars, discarded washing machines, plastic bags of trash in the dooryard.

Chuckie was slow to get out of the car. When I returned two days later, he was uncommunicative, sullen, unusually (even for Chuckie) slow to follow directions. *YOU'RE NOT THE BOSS OF ME.* And all too often, it would take three burly Associates (they were called) to keep him from smashing windows, pissing on the furniture like a dog in a junkyard.

On those days, I grew especially fond of Chuckie. There was a sweetness in him underneath all the rage. His drive to survive made him a hero in my eyes. A superhero. Even today, in the face of rude and petty officialdom, I hear Chuckie's voice and I whisper for only myself to hear, *You're not the boss of me.*

LIKE A BOLT OF LIGHTNING

Picture a great, magnificent hemlock, just up the ridge from her house. One night, the tree was struck by lightning, an ear-splitting crash, and, in the morning, the tree was shattered, huge splinters driven into the ground, like bolts of the lightning itself.

Years later...this young girl, Maddie, who played the violin and read so voraciously... Why she was in this home for lost children was hard to make sense of, a question more of custody than behavior, it would seem.

And then one afternoon, working in the woods (community service, it was called), another tree shattered by lightning in a storm the night before. Huge shards driven into the ground.

Maddie wrapped her arms around the splintered trunk and whispered to the tree in an attempt to console it.

And that night, Maddie slipped from her bed, slipped past the not-so-watchful eyes of her guardians, and made her way through the night towards a place she remembered as home.

Someone gave her a ride, this lost child, and someone else dropped her off on a winding road through the mountains. Maddie walked slowly up the road, feeling the edge of the pavement with her feet. She did not hear the car approaching up the hill and around the corner behind her.

Suddenly, screeching tires, blinding lights, bolting from the darkness...

And then... the driver of the car, a young woman herself, a nurse at the hospital nearby, standing in the rain, weeping over the lifeless body at her feet.

SECOND CHOICE

The dream recurs. The woman, the goats, the pines in the moonlight. Even now, ten years later, the images are vivid and clear. But she was *not* a dream. She was not a dream, and I have a photograph to prove it. Forwarded to me by a certain Ms. Greenfield, no return address, locked now in a drawer in my desk, it shows *her*, just as she was— brown from the sun, standing on her doorstep, laughing, earrings dangling like the ears of the goats in the pasture. Never, under any circumstances, must I let Marjorie see the photograph. Several times I have thought to destroy it. Why do I cling to it so? As I'll say again later, there is a great deal about this story that I do not understand.

Now, my thoughts wander, drift back all those years to a humid, overcast day in late April. It all seemed so routine, so mundane, at the time. I had spent the better part of the morning driving north from Boston. In my pocket was a carefully annotated list of lakeshore cottages available for rental during the month of August. "Just the kind of vacation we need," Marjorie had contended, "a chance for all of us to just relax and get to know each other again."

And she was right, of course. It had been a bad year for us, especially with the kids, both of them, Jimmy and Renee. Jimmy was flunking Algebra and had been caught smoking marijuana on his way home from school. Marjorie said it was all she could do to put up with him at home. Both of them: Renee, only a year younger, had grown as rude and sullen as her brother.

For my own part, I had little to do with it all. For several years, my work at the Agency had absolutely overwhelmed me. Even this vacation was difficult to justify; when I speak of "spending" time, I mean it literally. But perhaps Marjorie was right. "Priorities," she said. She herself had grown increasingly withdrawn and bitter; our evenings of intimacy were a thing of the past. In fact, to be honest, I could recall numerous evenings when I had returned to the office after supper just to escape her naggings and complainings.

But, as I said, perhaps Marjorie was right; perhaps this vacation would be a good thing for all of us—though, in fairness, I must admit that I saw my own role quite simply as that of dutiful father. Only in retrospect can I see the conflicts that festered in me at the time—still fester, for that matter, with this difference: that now I see them clearly, know them well, acknowledge my powerlessness to do anything about them. Marjorie and I settle through the years like soot down a chimney, joined now in a shared downdraft. Only I, the one-time romantic, am haunted by sparks and embers from the past.

In any case, we had argued. Marjorie had prevailed; we would rent a cottage on a lake for the month of August. Now, as I drove through the countryside of southern Maine, I recalled the dozens of phone calls to real estate agents, the maps on the dining room table, the scores of listings, crosshatched with penciled comments and descriptions. And I recalled this: the night almost a month earlier when we had sat at the table, the kids refusing to participate, and pared the list down to the six possibilities I now carried in my pocket. There had been a sense of shared purpose in the endeavor, a sense of long forgotten closeness. Later that night, kids gone to bed, Marjorie had fetched a bottle of brandy, and we had stayed up talking. Afterwards, for the first time ever, we had made love downstairs, there on the dining room carpet. In the morning, I had showered and slipped away to the office, feeling slightly hungover and foolish. The incident had not repeated itself.

Now, on this particular weekend in late April, it was my appointed job to conduct a personal investigation of the six rental possibilities. Renee had almost come with me but had opted at the last minute for a roller skating party with her friends. Marjorie was involved for the weekend with one women's group or another, and Jimmy, off probation at last, was tied up with pre-season baseball practices. It all seemed so routine and familiar to me. By the time I pulled into the little town of Gray, I was feeling slightly disoriented. Business trips I was used to, with their pre-arranged meetings and accommodations. But this was different; it was years since I'd been off on my own like this, exploring, essentially. Yes, as I said, it was disorienting, but also, in some obscure way, edgy and exciting. Somewhere, I would have to find a room for the night.

At the Gray Realty Office, Hiram Gray himself drove me to a little place on something called Fillmore Lake, five miles from the center of town. Our second choice the night of the brandy and Number Two on my annotated list, the cottage itself was perfect with its three bedrooms, the deck over the lake, the secluded, pine-scented lot. All were precisely as we had envisioned, perhaps a bit newer-looking, a bit more modern, but that would suit Marjorie perfectly. The sailboat, stored under the deck would, presumably, keep the kids interested and occupied. That was our hope, in any case. All this I told Mr. Gray on the ride back to town. I thanked him for his trouble and promised to be in touch.

The third, fourth, fifth, and sixth places on our list all

sounded similar to the first, though none so secluded and none with a boat. All were farther north up the turnpike. Our first choice, however, Number One on our list... In retrospect, I'm astonished that we included it at all. An island, the realtors had said, short boat ride offshore; honeymoon cottage; one bedroom and sleeping porch for kids. Little farmstead nearby with fresh eggs and milk from the goats. Egads! What were we thinking? Marjorie needed everything from the supermarket and wrapped in plastic. Maybe it was the headiness of that evening with the brandy. Maybe we ranked this place so high as a little joke almost, a whimsy we would indulge before getting on with the business of our real selection.

I drove northward in a funk, and the landscape became increasingly rural. As I approached the town of Greenfield, my impatience was simmering. An island, for god's sake! Kids sleeping on the *porch?* That would go over great with Jimmy. How in god's name...? Hunger gnawed at my stomach. I pulled off the road and reached for the picnic basket Marjorie had packed the night before: ham sandwiches, lukewarm beer, a crumbled macaroon for dessert. Outside the car, a meadow sloped away to a farm in the valley below. Thrushes sang in the hedgerow. I finished my sandwiches, closed my eyes, soothed by the beer, dozing and listening. When I opened my eyes, perhaps ten minutes later, a herd of black and white cows had congregated nearby. They stood along the fence, motionless, watching me with large, liquid eyes. I hadn't even *seen* a cow since I was a boy, and there thirteen or so of them stood, not six feet away, staring at me.

Not seen a cow since I was a boy? Not been alone like this on a country road since when? Ever? I rolled down the window and leaned out. I could not resist. "Mooo," I called. The cows did not respond. "Mooo," I called louder. And with that moo, I began to laugh. Oh what the heck; might as well check out the place on the island; no harm in that.

At Greenfield Real Estate Offices, only the receptionist was present, sloppily dressed and sprawled in a chair. Lisa Greenfield, it said on a plaque on her desk. The others were gone, she said; they had expected me sooner. I tried to explain about my dozing off by the roadside, about the cows in the pasture, and I felt my impatience returning. Suddenly, this all seemed so silly. What was I even doing here?

But Ms. Greenfield just smiled and continued. She *could* close the office and come with me, she said. Or (and she emphasized the word) I could go on my own. She could give me directions and the key. Only don't disturb the owner on the other side of the island; she preferred to remain in the background, to have nothing to do with the rental. Just drop the key through the mail slot on my way back through town.

I vacillated, aware that Ms. Greenfield was watching me closely. "As I said," she began, "I could come ..." But then she seemed to change her mind. She went back to writing out directions and drawing lines on a map.

As I said at the outset, there is a great deal about this story that I do not understand. Or, if I understand it today, I did not understand it then. I do know this much however: that today a cottage on an island would not even be under consideration. And I myself would not be off trekking through the countryside on such a ridiculous mission. But this was back then, ten years ago; my questing for adventure and profundity in life had not expired altogether.

160

I took the key from Ms. Greenfield, and I carefully folded the directions she had written out. "Just drop the key in the mailslot on your way back through town," she called after me. "We'll get it on Monday."

For the next ten minutes or so, I cruised north on the Interstate. It was good, a necessary interlude, allowing me to regain some sense of control. Turnpikes, airports, chain motels and restaurants, these were familiar territory. Here, at least, cows did nor invade one's privacy; the Ms. Greenfields of the world did not lounge about bra-less at ancient roll-top desks, toy, teasingly it seemed, with the idea of accompanying one to remote honeymoon cottages. What had changed her mind anyway? She seemed so casual, loose, off-handed. I caught a glimpse of myself in the rearview mirror. Youthful enough, I thought. A bit tired around the eyes. No more than ten years her senior. Perhaps a bit too buttoned-down and well-groomed, a certain tightness to the chin and lips. "Oh come on, Dad," I could almost hear my kids say, "don't be so uptight."

What a word that is – *uptight*. Impossible to deal with. In fact, it seemed the more one tried to deal with it, the more uptight one became. I glanced at the face in the mirror again. No, there was nothing wrong with the face. A certain ruddiness lacking, of course, but nothing a few hours of sunshine wouldn't cure. Perhaps a certain listlessness, lack of sparkle, radiance, what did they call it, charisma. But then I *was* tired; it had been a long day, a long week, a long winter.

EXIT 7 – One Mile. I caught the sign in the corner of my eye. My hands tensed a bit on the steering wheel, then relaxed as I rounded the curve of the exit ramp and headed west. Two-lane traffic now and greening pastures with herds of cattle. I turned the rearview mirror to face me; the eyes in the mirror stared back at me. "Moo," I said tauntingly, veering dangerously close to the roadside ditch. I spun the wheel in time; the face in the mirror was grinning.

Six miles from the Exit, Ms. Greenfield's instructions said. Watch for a dirt road to the left and go two miles down that. Watch closely for a little road off that through the pines, more of a passageway really. There will be a chain across that; the larger of your two keys will unlock the chain. Watch out for mud. At the end of the road, you will come to the lake. You can see the island a hundred yards or so out, and the roof of the cottage. There should be a dinghy pulled up on the shore. If not, you'll have to blow your horn, but she won't be too happy about that.

Watch out for the mud! Ms. Greenfield's instructions were complete—with one exception: what to do if I found the mud. Twenty minutes from the Interstate, with the mid-afternoon sun beating on my head, I found myself sunk to the hubcaps in thick, oozing mud. In frustration, I sat in the car and blasted the horn, long, insistent blasts, demanding attention. All I wanted by that point was to get out of there, get back to the Interstate, eat somewhere, find a clean motel for the night, drop off the keys in the morning, call Hiram Gray and return home. I had found the perfect place, I would tell Marjorie: secluded, modern, three bedrooms, even a sailboat under the porch. What about the others, Marjorie would ask. No point in wasting time on those, I would tell her, and that would end it. Deep questioning was a thing of the past with Marjorie.

For half an hour or so, I sat in the car, periodically blasting the horn. I contemplated hiking out to the main road and calling a wrecker; that was the reasonable thing to do, the obvious, sane course of action. But somehow... the long walk, the foolishness of my predicament... perhaps on the island there would be something, a winch of sorts or, what did they call it, a cumalong? Inexplicably in retrospect, I pushed on. I locked my car and launched the dinghy.

A honeymoon cottage, the realtor had called it, though Ms. Greenfield had referred to it simply as a camp. It stood atop a grassy knoll on the landward side of the island. Across the island, presumably, hidden from me now, would be the little farm. In retrospect again, my thinking was anything but clear, as I beached the dinghy and ascended the knoll. Obviously, my number one concern should have been getting my car out of the mud. Towards that end, I needed equipment. But other forces were at work too. Yes, I was looking for tools, but while I was about it, I might as well check out the cottage. Could there have been a lingering desire to please Marjorie, to have a story for her, to answer the follow-up questions she no longer asked? More than that, could there have been still, at that time of my life, a lingering voyeuristic curiosity? This was a honeymoon cottage after all. On an island, not to mention this business of the anonymous owner. Who was she, anyway? As I said, all of the above, none of the above, something drew me on. I climbed the knoll towards the cottage.

I did not find, did not really expect to find, block and tackle waiting for me on the porch. In fact, barring some wicker furniture, some cups on a shelf, an old brass bedstead, the cottage was empty. I stood in the doorway and recorded the essentials: whatever else, I *would* have answers. One bedroom, one large all-purpose room with gas lights, refrigerator, and stove. No indoor plumbing, hand pump at the sink, outhouse visible through the bedroom window. Nice view of the lake on three sides. All very clean and freshly painted. Even a little vase of flowers on a windowsill, and a curtain billowing in the breeze.

At the sink, just testing, mind you, I worked the handle of the pump. Brilliantly clear, ice-cold water gushed from the spout. Mesmerized, I pumped and pumped some more, stopping at last to fill a glass. I retreated to the porch and sank into a newly-caned rocking chair. I would rest for a minute, sip my water, gather my thoughts.

Before me, the meadow sloped down to the lake. In the summer, no doubt, it would be filled with wildflowers; roses and hollyhocks would climb the trellises on the sides of the cottage. All in all, I recall thinking, even at that time of my life, that it was a tremendous cliche. And yet, there it was, and, if there was any meaning left to the word, it was an idyllic spot, a honeymoon cottage in every sense of the word, something from a fairy tale or a children's story, far removed from the realities of everyday life. Only the honeymooners were missing, foolish, innocent children, brown from the sun, infused with their passion, making their love at all hours of the day, sitting for long, lingering evening hours on the porch, asking and answering a lifetime of questions, sleeping sweetly and waking to blueberry muffins, lovingly tendered, reveling in their soft, silly puppy love. I recalled once bringing Marjorie blueberry muffins in bed, calling in sick for work, and believing for years afterwards that the sullen, brooding Jimmy owed his conception to that morning.

A cooling breeze rose from the lake, riffling the grasses

in the meadow. The tinkling of windchimes on the porch brought me back to my senses. Priorities! My investigations! Honeymoon cottage out of the question too small, no plumbing. Rentals three through six still pending. All irrelevant now; car up to its hubcaps in mud, Stuck. I would have to cross the island and seek help at the farm. Odd in retrospect that I did not even consider what was still my best option: return to the mainland, hike out to the state highway, and call a wrecker. There was still plenty of time before dark. But no, as I keep saying, there is much about this story that I do not understand. Instead, I would cross the island and seek help at the little farm.

Behind the cottage, a forest of virgin pine sprawled at the center of the island. From shore, it had looked like the quilled back of a giant porcupine. A beaten path wound, cave-like in places, through the pines. Late afternoon sun sliced through the branches, blinding at times, casting a reddish glow on the dark trunks. The sun itself, through some optical trick, burned round and red at the end of a long tunnel through the trees. The path curved to the left; the sun was over my shoulder now, and I felt a bit disoriented by the slashing light and shifting shadows.

Just a few hundred yards, according to Ms. Greenfield. And yet, padding along on a thick carpet of pine needles, sunlight knifing through the branches, surreal in its effects, tired now from the long day, definitely disoriented, knowing only that I needed help to get my car out, that help might be available at the little farm, those facts advancing and receding like fits of nausea, it might have been more than a few hundred yards, much more. I was emotionally exhausted. As I've said, I hadn't been off on my own like this in years, unstructured, finding my own way through the forest.

More like half a mile it was. I emerged from the forest at the top of a grassy hillside. Below me lay a large meadow, bordered by the forest, bordered along the lakefront, hidden from the lake in fact, by a row of towering ancient pines. The tops of the trees glowed reddish-gold in the late afternoon sun. The meadow itself was an island, an island in the forest, an island within an island in a lake in a forest—a Chinese box within a box within other boxes...

At the far end of the meadow, half-nestled into the forest, was the *little farm*, seven or eight structures, animal shelters presumably, clustered and presided over by a small, low, bungalow-style cottage. All were neatly shingled, weathered to a gray sheen, highlighted by freshly-painted, deep maroon trim. Nearby, a sapling fence enclosed perhaps a quarter of the meadow. Inside the pasture, a dozen or so goats had stopped their browsing and were standing expectantly, their drooping ears lifted slightly, gazing up at me. Behind them, at the threshold of the bungalow, a human figure, a woman apparently, stood gazing also, her hand cupped against the sunlight.

Again, as earlier in the day, this feeling of being confronted by a cliché, something so hackneyed and irrelevant as to no longer be real. I had never seen such a place before—only in storybooks. Yet, unless I was exhausted, drained to the point of dreaming, the place was real. I waved to the figure in the doorway and started down the hillside.

Baa-aa-aa. As I approached the pasture, the goats broke their silence and rushed to greet me. Long, droopy-eared creatures they were with Roman noses, jostling about, following on their side of the fence as I circled the pasture.

Baa-aa. I stopped to watch. The goats stretched towards me through the fence. Something in their eyes—not the docile, liquid patience of the cows, but something bright, playful, intelligent. Something in their baaings, too—not the mournful mooings of the cows, but something quick and alive.

"They're Nubians," called the woman. Something in her voice, too, in her throat, on the verge of laughter. She was sitting on the stoop now, long skirt tucked around her knees, chin cupped in her hand, watching me. I turned back to the goats. "Baa-aa-aa," I called.

The woman continued to watch me from her stoop. I walked over and sat beside her, lounged really, still chuckling, with my elbows on the step behind me. The woman's eyes, above the knuckles of her hand, were laughing, as if secretly enjoying my performance, my befuddlement. No, not secretly enjoying, as if openly sharing. And here, on her doorstep, I had collapsed without introduction.

"I heard you honking," the woman said. Her eyes were averted, and she was plucking at grass shoots between the stones of the doorstep. "I couldn't come. It's kidding time for the goats, and Columbine needed my help."

Kidding time for the goats? Columbine? I remembered my insistent honking, blasting away, demanding attention. Who was that man? That angry man? I remembered Ms. Greenfield, the abrupt change in her manner. Now I felt trapped, trapped by something far more gripping than the mud up to my hubcaps. No, my top priority now, more important than any vacation cottage or stuck car was this: for once in my life, not to appear *uptight*, not to *be* uptight. For my own sake. On the stoop of this odd little bungalow, beside this strange, laughing-eyed woman, something inside me was stirring.

The woman was watching me. She whistled softly. "Wake up," she said. "It's all right. I named them Mudpie and Toot." She laughed. "Mudpie and Toot. Two beautiful does. All brown, like their father."

I glanced at her. Briefly again, the eyes sparkling above the knuckles, before she turned away and gazed out over the lake. I saw now what a handsome woman she was: straight profile, almost classical; skin brown from the sun; red bandanna; gold hoop earrings; shoulders squared; girlish in some ways, but older than she had seemed—mid-thirties to early forties, anywhere in there. And an impression of abstraction now; she had drifted away, saddened, yes, an aura of sadness. And with that, a sense of timelessness, as if she, we, had been sitting there, would be sitting there, always. She seemed in absolutely no hurry, suspended almost in time and space. No nervous fluttering, no getting on with her work, no offering of food or drink, no pressing on with the details of my predicament. The sense of an unmoving, unchanging here-and-now was total – and infectious. The minutes drifted by. Perhaps I felt it was already too late to do anything about my car. More than that, it didn't really seem to matter anymore. We watched the glow disappear from the tops of the pines. From a faint little saltbox of a barn came the muffled bleatings of the goats.

"Mudpie," I mused at last. "How did you know I was stuck in the mud?" My words came slowly, sing-song and oddly inflected.

The woman turned from the lake, smiling broadly, her eyes mocking. "Didn't *you* know?" she asked. But it was gentle mockery. Again the feeling that she was sharing something with me.

I laughed. "I *do* have to get out," I said, surprising myself with the emphasis, as if perhaps an alternative had been offered, as if perhaps I did *not* have to get out.

The woman was silent, plucking at the grass at her feet. When she spoke, her words were soft and serious, barely audible. "There's a path around the lake," she said. "If you follow it up the hill from your car—not very far, just a few minutes—you'll come to a little house. An old man lives there. Harold. Used to own this island; built this farm, the cottage. He lives there year round now. He's got a Jeep." She paused, still plucking at the grass, then added, "He's very kind; he'll pull you out."

Again there was silence, except for the soft bleatings from the barn. "Now?" I asked abruptly. "He'll pull me out now?"

"He's very kind," the woman repeated.

I shivered. The chill of twilight had crept over the meadow. The pines along the shore were towering, dark sentries. I half-expected a full moon to rise over the lake, to illuminate the pastoral little scene, to complete the cliché, such as it was. And it was with that thought, that flash of irony, that, suddenly, I was swept under. Wave after wave of fatigue, muscle-aching exhaustion, mind-numbing world-weariness washed over me. The thought of walking back across the island, rowing to shore, finding Harold, dealing with the mud, strange restaurants and motels... No, my palms burned from the rowing; I had come too far; I had come too far. I buried my face in my hands, and, for the first time since... Since when? Ever? I wept. Only distantly did I hear the woman's voice: "...soup, tea,

169

something for my blistering hands? Inside..."

Dazed, mortified, angry at myself for appearing so pathetic, yet unable to stop, pull myself together, regain that threshold of benign amusement I had experienced just minutes ago, like a sick puppy-dog, I followed her into the cottage and collapsed into a rocking chair at a low table. I could not speak; craven apologies stuck in my throat. Dumbly, I watched the woman move about her bungalow, closing windows, lighting kerosene lanterns.

My hostess, as she now was, knelt by the low table beside me, smiling, prying the lid off a a small green can, her eyes soft in the flickering light. "Stop worrying," she said. "Everything's going to be all right." Laughter again in her voice—and again that feeling that she was not evaluating, judging, just accepting whatever might happen and coping with kindness. She placed the can on the table in front of me. *Bag Balm,* it said on the label. Dumbly working the salve into my blisters, I continued to watch her, brewing tea now, ladling soup from a crock-pot on a wood-burning kitchen range. She brought two bowls to the table and sat across from me. Wordlessly, we spooned our soup—thick leek soup, laden with herbs and spices—and tore chunks of bread off a freshly-baked loaf. Once, spoon lifted, I glanced up and caught her eye. Her spoon, too, was lifted, poised under her nose. We both laughed—some conspiracy afoot. Except I had no idea what I was laughing about—always one had to laugh at something, never for the sake of laughter itself, as seemed to be the case with this woman. And it was infectious; I could not keep from smiling, grinning inside, as she later put it.

And then, abruptly, in the wake of the laughter, the trap closed on me again. What in god's name was I doing here;

my position was absurd, my laughter hollow. Aware that the woman was watching me, I finished my soup with my eyes on my spoon, looked up only when the bowl was lifted from the table and a mug of strong, herbal tea steamed in its place. I glanced at her face again—not laughing now but sad, contemplative, weighted with compassion. How I despised myself then—for becoming the object of such pity, for deadening the laughter in her eyes. Again, the craven apologies stuck in my throat.

"The tea will be good for you," the woman said simply. Compliantly, I sipped from the mug. Soon, she was only a shadow, moving soundlessly about the bungalow. Then her voice again— something about going out to milk the goats. I dozed in my chair. Only later did I wonder just what magical herbs had been brewed into my tea.

I awoke several hours later to the sound of loud, insistent bleatings from the goat barn. Cool night air swept through the bungalow and brought me groping to my senses. I felt wonderfully relaxed and clear-headed. Something was obviously happening in the goat barn; the front door of the bungalow was ajar on its hinges; my hostess was apparently in the barn already. Like a sleepwalker, I slipped from the bungalow, closing the door behind me.

Outside, a full moon had risen and illuminated the meadow. Shadows from the big pines played across the pasture and the little cluster of buildings. A square of light fell from the window of the goat barn and lay distinct and motionless on the ground. The bleatings of the goats had given way to grunts and muted baa-ings. I moved through the moonlight, feeling, I recall, calm, slightly detached, like a visitor from a different world, a *real* world, wandering about an abandoned stage set. Except, for all its storybook charm and moonlit mystery, this was not a stage set; in its way, it was as real as anything I'd ever experienced. And it was not abandoned. From the barn now, came the sounds of the woman's voice, soft, soothing. "Steady there, Colly. It's all right, it's all right now..."

Inside the little barn, she was kneeling in the hay, her arm up to the elbow inside a large black-and-tan doe. Lantern light fell across her face, the pained, compassionate face I had seen before, set now in its determination. "Easy now, Colly..." Slowly, she began to withdraw her arm. The goat began to call softly, as if coaxing something from her own body; then she crouched, pushing and bawling loudly. With one sure movement, my hostess withdrew her hand, easing the third, the stillborn kid, from the body of its mother. The doe called softly again, then began to lick her kid clean. Abruptly, she stopped and gazed up at the woman. "It's all right, Colly," the woman said. She rubbed the doe's forehead with her knuckles. I could not see her face as she lifted the kid from the hay and placed it in a grain bag. Only then did she turn to me, smiling, that incredible smile, sharing everything. "It happens," she said. "I should have expected triplets."

"My honking...." I started to say. Again, the trap closing. Me caught between two selves, cravenly apologizing for one, powerless to sustain the other.

"You couldn't have known," the woman said. "How *could* you have known?" Something in the way she spoke, the tone of her voice, her inflection, her emphasis. How *could* I have known? Any word in her question might have been stressed; it could have been a demand or an accusation. But this woman in her goat barn, my hostess as

172

she was, spoke only understanding and forgiveness. How *could* I have known? In her eyes, the world was blameless. Things happened, and it was all right. Now, she would take care of the afterbirth; could I fetch some warm water from the stovetop, mix up a mash for Columbine?

Never have I worked with such joy, such immersion in my task, such a deep sense of purpose. And I say this quite objectively, without irony or self pity, because never again will I experience, allow myself to experience, such a state of transcendence, such a state of altered reality. Just moments before, I'd been feeling trapped, filled with self-disgust. Perhaps it was the tea the woman had served me—obviously cannabis was among its herbal ingredients—but I had swung wildly from one emotional extreme to the other. I could have mixed mash there forever.

In the bungalow again, I sat in my rocking chair, clinging to the remnants of my mood. At the stove, my hostess, Anne she told me her name was, busied herself brewing another pot of tea. Her back seemed less straight now, weary, her movements slow. For the first time, I noticed the finely-crafted cabinetry above her head, the low, thick-beamed ceiling. The bungalow was lit only by softly glowing kerosene lanterns. Shelves everywhere were filled with books, colorful jars, small wood carvings of creatures of the forest. Tapestries hung on the walls and covered the doorway to a back room—her bedroom, I guessed. I sipped tea now. In a trance, it seemed, I noticed the heavy, carved front door with its wrought iron hinges and latch—the same door I had closed so thoughtfully only a few hours earlier. I marveled at the craftsmanship, the texture of the materials, the way everything flowed together. Then my thoughts turned inwards. I marveled at my own newfound capacity for wonder—as if a new way of seeing had opened up to me, a capacity for calm, unhurried perception and appreciation. Even the sounds of the bungalow seemed profound: the lid clinking on the teapot, the sounds of Anne's footfalls—they sounded old, old as the darkened beams overhead—her voice, suddenly cheerful and young. "Don't worry about your car," she said. "Harold will help you in the morning."

My car! Space junk abandoned on Mars. Her words seemed brittle, disconnected, and yet, like everything else about her, profound and fraught with hidden meaning. She sat in the shadows across the table from me. In silence, we sat sipping our tea. Thoughts of Marjorie popped up, home by herself with the kids. How would I explain this to her, this sitting on this remote doorstep with this mysterious woman? This feeling of profound contentment...? When I spoke at last, my own voice had the sound of a cello I had played once as a child, deep and sonorous. I asked her who she was, where she had come from. Was there a story behind this laughing-eyed, enigma of a woman?

"Oh god," she said, "we'd be up half the night. You'd oversleep and miss Harold."

"Please," I said. "I want to know." Deep notes on my cello. Something was eluding me, something vital, essential. I *had* to know.

In the silence, she refilled our teacups. When she spoke, her voice was soft, barely audible. I remember just fragments today. Born in Philadelphia. Best schools; master's degree in anthropology. Vacation in Maine. Met Simon Greenfield, heir to thriving real estate business. Young, innocent, idealistic; stupidly married; didn't last through the honeymoon.

I remember the feeling of her watching me from the shadows. Something resonated. "Honeymoon?" I asked her. "Where did you go for your honeymoon?"

Again silence. Then, softly prodding, "Where do you think? Simon Greenfield?"

I slapped my forehead. "It was just the way it is today," she said. "We swam and played, talked a lot, pretended we were in paradise, the first people on earth. That lasted about a week. Afterwards, we went our separate ways."

I listened, entranced. And I told her about my own marriage, our honeymoon in Bermuda. We pretended a lot, I told her. We were not very honest with each other. We spent a week in a hotel full of honeymooning couples. We just did what everyone else did—talked a lot about my career, the house we would buy...

Across the table, I could see her rocking almost imperceptibly, gazing down at her hands in her lap. "That's where it all fell apart for me," she said. "There was nothing there. I walked away from it all. Literally, I walked away..."

I will never forget my response, never know for sure whether it was the highpoint of self-awareness, or the bedrock of self-deception. "You were lucky," I said. "You were aware of alternatives; you knew you had choices."

Laughter again in her voice now, that hint of a Mona Lisa smile. "And you didn't?" she asked. "We always have choices."

I tried to laugh with her, but the deep vibration was gone from my voice. Something was changing. I felt as though I were awakening from a dream and could not recapture it. She leaned forward in her chair. Again that smile, the laughter and sadness mixed in her eyes. Almost playfully, she brushed my arm with her hand. "You're tired," she said. "I'll get you a pillow. You can sleep on the couch."

The straightness of her back—I remember that as she fetched bedding from a closet and spread it on a sofa under the windows, as she paused at the curtain separating us from a sleeping room for herself. What seemed like a shiver ran across her shoulders. "Sleep now," she said. "Everything will be fine in the morning. Buenas noches, my poor stuck-in-the-mud friend."

Again, that sensation of a dream fading, of light, warmth, reality itself dwindling. I felt so alone, so abandoned. Never have I yearned so much for anything as I yearned to be with her then – the warmth, the closeness, the sense of fullness I had experienced earlier. I felt drawn, like a moth to light.

But I did not move from my sofa. What held me there? What fear? What anxiety? Why could I not simply go to this woman, confident and alive as herself? Why? Would I offend her in some way? Would some tone in my voice, some look in my eye, expose me as a fraud, a phony, a pretender at this game of life? Yes, I had mooed at the cows in the pasture; what a paltry effort that had been. Now, I knew exactly what I wanted to do, what I wanted to be. Never had I hated myself so much. I could not sleep.

It was then that the woman returned. She sat on the edge of the sofa. "Roll over," she said softly. She began to knead the knots in my shoulders. Gradually, I abandoned control, gave myself over to the kneading of her fingers. I would not fight sleep; I had nothing to offer this woman— not then and probably never. I would let her nurse me; I would let her croon and rub my back until I fell asleep. In the morning, I would return to my responsibilities.

Everything would be all right then. She had assured me..

In the morning, there was a note on the table. "Coffee and oatmeal on the stove," it said. "Harold will help you with your car." I helped myself to breakfast, feeling remarkably rested and alert. My hostess, my angel and hostess, was nowhere in sight.

At the lakefront, the dinghy was gone. In its place, a small kayak was tied to the dock. A green can of Bag Balm squatted on the dock nearby. I worked the salve into the palms of my hands and lowered myself into the kayak. A few hundred yards away, I could see movement on shore— a green Jeep hooked to my car, a large man with a flowing white beard, striding about purposefully with a shovel, my beautiful hostess from the night before, watching me approach in the kayak.

"Buenos dias," she called out as I drew closer. "Good morning, my poor stuck-in-the-mud friend." As always it seemed, the lilting laughter in her voice, the rich timbre. I beached my kayak and slogged through the mud to my car. "This is Harold," my hostess said. Harold's hand engulfed mine. He had a flowing beard and tufted eyebrows over radiantly blue eyes. "Now you get in your car, Sonny," he told me. "You put 'er in reverse, and when you feel me pullin' you give 'er some gas."

Harold knew what he was doing. Just a minute or two later we were all standing on high ground, my car idling nearby. Harold was shaking my hand again. "Now you be careful what you get yourself into, Sonny," he said, winking at me. And my beautiful hostess just smiled that smile of hers and shook her head sadly. She hugged me briefly. "Be good to yourself, my friend" was all she said.

Back at the offices of Simon Greenfield, Realtor, the

young woman was there by herself again. She greeted me warmly. "Have an experience?" she asked teasingly. Something about the sound of her words, the laughter in her voice. "Yes," she said, "She was my mother. She *is* my mother." She paused, drew a deep breath. "Would you like some coffee? Maybe a bagel with some cheese? Goat cheese, that would be..." Her eyes twinkled.

And then Ms. Greenfield, Lisa Greenfield that was, told me her story—how her mother, well-educated and 'from away,' and Simon Greenfield had met, foolishly gotten married, spent a week at the Honeymoon Cottage (thank god for that, she noted, otherwise...), and then gone their separate ways. Her mother had bought the little farm from Harold, who had once owned the island, built the cottage, carved the little farm itself out of the forest. He was a fine woodsman, a fine artist and carpenter, half a generation older than her mom but hale and hearty as an old goat. In fact, he was often part of the household when she herself was there during the summers; she remembered him fondly. She herself had been raised in town by her father and his family and had studied business management in school and hoped to take over the real estate offices one of these days. At this point she reached into a drawer in her desk and withdrew a photo, a picture of her mother standing in the door of her bungalow, brown from the sun, laughing, the same picture I have buried in my own desk drawer to this day. "You can keep this," she said. "Something about her. Siren songs, whatever. Men do seem to like her." She drew another deep breath. "I guess you won't be renting the cottage..."

As I keep saying, so much about this story I don't understand. I left the office feeling...what? Reconciled I think would be the word, accepting of myself and my role in life. As I passed the roadside turnout where I had wolfed down my sandwich and moo-ed at the cows just twenty-four hours earlier, I pulled off the road briefly. Cows drifted in my general direction. I did not roll down my window; I did not even look at the cows. I would call Hiram Gray on my way through town, reserve the little cottage with the sailboat under the deck, return home where I belonged.

And now, today, all these years later, I don't even remember what stories I concocted for Marjorie. She loved my descriptions of the cottage with the sailboat. Our vacation week there was a disaster, with the kids grousing and bickering and sheets of rain lashing at the windows. It was the last "family vacation" we attempted, and the kids talk about it today like some illness we all suffered together. Both in college now, with lives of their own, they rarely come home. Marjorie misses them, wonders where we "went wrong" as a family. She busies herself with her various clubs and initiatives around town. I'm a senior partner at the Agency now, struggling with car and mortgage payments, tuition for the kids, haunted at times by images from the past. Somewhere, I have a key to the drawer in my desk, to the photograph of the woman with the husky voice and the laughing eyes. Yes, a key, with other keys and marbles, coins and assorted paraphernalia in an old shoebox, I believe, on a shelf in the basement.

PART III –
THE VIEW FROM MY
TREEHOUSE

(I am in a little room I've constructed for myself upstairs in what we call a barnlet attached to our home in Maine. I call this room my treehouse. Just out my window, a giant oak tree towers over the cars in the driveway. This morning, the branches are festooned with new leaves unfurling for the summer months ahead. Soon, my view will be blocked, and I will listen to the rustling of leaves, but, in October and November, the leaves will fall, revealing once again the hills and rivers in the distance, and the valleys with their towns, and their people with their never-ending stories.)

A TSUNAMI OF TURKEYS

Good grief...
Working in my little treehouse retreat this morning,
And glancing out the window
Just then...
A flock of wild turkeys
Marching up the street,
Strutting their stuff
Now that Thanksgiving Day is behind them.
Strong image,
Those turkeys just outside my window.
Like all the deer under
The apple trees outback
Day after hunting season is over.
And just a few minutes later,
Roar of plow truck
Barreling down the street
Pushing a veritable
Tsunami-of-slush on its blade.
Probably got a few of those
Strutting turkeys.
Caught up in the mix.
Like safe-at-last deer
Jacked out of season,
Or those migrant families at the border,
Free at last
From the hardships at home,
Dreaming of a safe future
In a new land,
Cut down instead
By tear gas at the crossing,

Separation from their children,
Watchful now for hunters
Out of season
And plow trucks bearing down
With slush blades akimbo.

(First published in *Goose River Anthology 2019*, Waldoboro, Maine)

GHOSTLY AROMAS

Some foul odor,
Sweetish, something decaying,
Wafting through the house.
First here, then there.
Impossible to pin down.
Last night, we tracked it for hours,
Sniffing at outlets,
Shining lights under cabinets.
We even moved the piano,
Nosing over its keyboard,
Poking into its cavities.
We found a business card.
Dragon's Breath Pottery,
And that seemed like a clue.
But it wasn't; we were baffled.
The smell eluded us,
Like some dream
Not to be captured,
Some olfactory will-o-the-wisp
This ghostly aroma,
Wafting through the house.
In the morning, we nailed it...
Months ago, kids at a workshop,
Coloring Easter eggs,
Instructor instructing all involved,
No, no need to hard-boil the eggs
Or blow out the innards.
Eggs will desiccate naturally
With no odor to be detected.
Oh such a mistruth that was,

Wandering in its own ghostly way
Through the hallways of science.
This bowl of eggs we found this morning,
Moved last night from the top of the piano,
Still brightly painted and lined so finely
In Ukrainian style,
Stank almost unbearably,
And the little puddle of liquid
Pooled at the bottom of the bowl
Was crawling with maggots.
Oh that was gross.
How we hadn't discovered it earlier
Was the new mystery of the morning.
So we took pictures of the eggs and the maggots,
And planned a new story for the children
About the elusiveness of truth,
And the importance of tracking down
The source of such things as
A bad smell in the house,
Or a piece of bad information from our teacher.

SKUNK WHISPERINGS

Gorgeous, silky fur - like those old pictures of Lassie. Or a foxtail I once saw, brushing the snow.

I'm standing well back, watching, focusing, using a two hundred millimeter lens to capture this creature. If it can be captured again, that is, captured as it is already, in this Have-a-Heart trap by the garden.

Pacing back and forth it is, rising up and pawing the sides of the trap.

We'd set the trap last night, placed arugula and peanut butter in a dish just beyond the trigger plate, hoping to catch a woodchuck we'd seen nibbling the perennials.

But this morning, no woodchuck, just this skunk pawing the side of the cage.

I talked to it as I snapped pictures, softly, reassuringly. (I'd been advised to do this by a skunk expert on Google.)

And I approached it, holding a blanket up by the corners, a curtain between myself and the skunk. (He won't spray you, if he can't see you, the experts had said.)

Moving slowly, talking softly, as if in a dance, I laid the blanket over the trap.

All was quiet; nothing moved. I wrapped the blanket around the ends of the trap, belted it in place with a bungee cord, carried it to my car, and drove Mr. Skunk to his new home at the Town Forest, where I was careful beyond careful, and whispering throughout, to keep the blanket always between us, as I struggled with the release gate on the trap.

(That was the only hard part, and my experts told me later to have a stick always handy in the future.)

But stick or no stick, I managed to prop the gate open,

and wait just about seven (I'd been told it would be eight) minutes before Mr. Skunk gathered his courage, sniffed the air, and ambled his way through meadow grasses to the edge of the forest.

I returned home – to my office, my treehouse, such as it is, where I admired the images I'd captured on my Canon EOS. And I resumed work on a children's story I'd been writing, a nature story, it was, told by me as a skunk whisperer.

And now in the story, it was the next day, and the clan were all gathered outside their burrow, wondering where in the world Uncle Harold had got to this morning.

ASSHOLES OF DEMOCRACY

At the Town Forest again this morning, by the kiosk in the parking lot, two super-friendly dogs come bounding from the woods, lapping at my face, wiggling against my knees.

I do my best to ignore them. I have a skunk in a trap in the trunk of my car. I'd captured it earlier that morning, neighborhood skunk-whisperer that I am now, and, with dogs bounding about me, I choose not to release it—quite yet.

Just then, a stout middle-aged woman comes double-poling up the pathway from the lake. *I see you've met Kayden and Lola,* she calls out.

Yes, I call back. *Friendly dogs they are.*

Discussion follows: The deer flies are fierce, she tells me. But she loves it here by the lake where her dogs can run free.

I point to a small poster on the kiosk: ALL DOGS MUST BE LEASHED.

Oh that, the woman snorts, and she adds, *Most dogs are just fine.*

But there is the occasional exception, I point out, ignoring at this point, Lola (I believe it is) squatting on my foot.

The woman snorts again. *That's the trouble with democracy,* she says. *One asshole ruins it for everyone else.*

Baffled by her logic, I mention the skunk in the trap in the trunk of my car. *It is hot in there*, I point out. *Would Kayden and Lola be okay if I released the skunk? Let it run free, as it were?*

The woman flaps her cheeks and snorts again twice.

She herds her dogs into a small Subaru, and leaves the forest in a cloud of dust. I wave half-heartedly.

Strange sounds issue forth from the trap in the trunk of my car.

FOUR BOYS ON BICYCLES

There – just outside my window,
Leaves full now on the great oak,
Racing up the road,
Up Harriman's Hill, they call it,
Silver Lake just visible from the top,
Four boys on bicycles,
Brothers it appears,
Ranging in age from twelve perhaps
Down to six, the youngest,
Pedaling frantically to keep up,
The others looking back over their shoulders,
Checking, making sure he is still there,
(*Watch out for your brother,*
Take care of your brother...)
And all four boys holding tight in their fists
Long fishing poles, bamboo,
Bobbing out over their handlebars.
But now, the youngest has stopped.
The hill is too much for him.
The others stop too, turn back,
Walk with their brother up the hill.
All four boys pushing their bicycles now,
Poles dancing
Out over handlebars,
Like antennae of insects,
Testing the roadway ahead,
Pointing the way up Harriman's Hill,
And on to The Big Ones
That lurk in the shadows
Of the lake just beyond.

CLEAN SLATE

Exactly THAT... a blank slate.
Just got here to my little writing loft,
Opened up a new document,
Like a new sheet of paper,
Or a fresh field of snow
When you ski out
From the shadows of the forest
On a crisp winter's day...
A blank slate... a clean slate,
Like the last day of school
With the summer months ahead
Or that feeling you had as a kid,
After you'd told the priest all your sins,
Like how you'd broken your sister's baseball bat,
Or dipped your brother's toothbrush
In the toilet.
And later, quite a bit later,
Touched yourself inappropriately,
Or wondered what it would feel like,
To touch the breasts of the girl
Sitting just in front of you in Algebra class.
Really bad stuff like that.
Proscribed in some parsing of
The Ten Commandments,
In some faraway council of elders.
But now, on this particular
Crisp winter's morning,
With this fresh field before me,
On this laptop such as it is.
It's time to set forth,

To leave tracks, such as they are,
In this fresh field of snow,
Put words, such as they are,
On this fresh sheet of paper.
Except, I just did.
So much for that fresh field of snow.
Bless you my son, the priest had said.
Go forth and sin no more.

VARYING HARE

Yesterday, we saw January naked.

We were in the Great Pond Mountain Wildlands, hiking
along the Valley Road.

The ground was soft and muddy in places.

Beech leaves rustled, sunlight splashed on russet, gold,
brown patches of forest floor.

Sounds, colors, smells – the entire landscape was
gorgeous, exotic, alien.

Something was wrong, terribly wrong. Never before had
the forest appeared so exposed, so unshrouded,

As it did here, now, in the middle of this month (the
natives called it) of the popping trees.

Just then, a large rabbit, white, a varying hare, bounded
across the road and zigged around boulders,

Zagged through patches of russet, gold, and brown in the
forest.

For long minutes we watched this creature, this bolt of
whiteness,

Like an errant ping-pong ball careering through the
forest.

Coyotes, owls, predators all, lurked in the shadows.

And we wondered about this great white rabbit.

Tens of thousands of years of evolution to develop this
seasonal camouflage...

And all for naught on this thawful winter's day.

HARSH SHROUD

It had snowed in the night,
Not the soft, gentle
Snows of Yesteryear,
But a harsh shroud
Windswept in
From some Arctic morgue.
Ash-gray was the sky,
Fields and hillsides
Scaled and sculpted in white,
That colorless all-color
As Ishmael saw it.
And then suddenly
As if sprung from the earth,
A red ball
Dipping and gliding
Across the horizon,
Dipping and gliding,
The head of a cross-country skier,
Watch cap red as a cherry,
Body lost in the grayness,
Only the swish-swish
Sounds of skis on the snow
And the red ball
Dipping and gliding,
Pulsing like life itself
Against the harsh
And shrouded landscape.

PAYPHONE AT SANDY POINT

There,
In the little town of Stockton Springs,
On a corner of a little outbuilding.
At the edge of a little parking lot,
On a wooded knoll,
Just above the long pebbled shore
Of the mighty Penobscot River,
Just there,
Like some relic from a bygone culture,
An old fashioned payphone.
Gleaming in the late afternoon sunlight.
There were four of us on that knoll
That wintry afternoon,
Three adults and a visiting grandchild.
Jessica, mother of the child,
Studied the relic,
Pulled out her own little high tech
Handheld device,
And dialed a number.
The relic rang,
Raucous in the stillness.
Answer it, Elia, one of us urged,
And the child picked up the receiver,
Put it to her ear.
Silly small talk ensued
Until the mother said,
You can hang up now, Elia.
The child held the phone in her hand
You can hang up now, Elia,
The mother repeated.

196

The child looked at her. Puzzled.
But mom, she pleaded,
I don't know HOW to hang up.
The adults looked at one another,
And burst out laughing.
The sun was setting over the river,
But a new age was dawning.

ON THE OPPOSITE SHORE

Excellent!
Two cars in the driveway this morning...
Driving down HappyTown Road
Past my brother's house
On the way to somewhere else...
We're going to leave him alone today... not stop in;
He's in the early innings (he would call it)
Of a new relationship,
And we wouldn't want to interrupt anything.
I asked him earlier how the relationship was going,
and if he'd be home that afternoon.
Well, he said, you know my blue Subaru...
I do, I said.
And my friend has a blue Volkswagen.
That's a good start, I thought.
If the Subaru is gone and the VW is at the house,
It probably means we've gone off to Bangor in my car.
I registered the information.
If both cars are there,
We're probably off on a walk around the neighborhood –
Or both in the house.
Okay I'd said.
If my car is there and the VW is gone,
It probably means we've gone over to Susan's house for
    the day..
Aha, I had thought, so her name is Susan.
But another thought had crossed my mind.
What if both cars are gone? I'd asked.
Will that mean you've had a big fight
and gone your separate ways?

He'd bristled. No way is that going to happen! he'd said.
Which is about as clear a declaration of attachment
As you're going to get from my brother.
He's good at math, and this coded talk works well for him.
"One if by land, and two if by sea..."
The Early Americans made good use of smoke signals,
And the later Navajos cracked codes for the military.
My brother is in good company,
And I'm happy for him today.
Not exactly lanterns in a belfry or smoke-puffs on the
    horizon,
But two cars in the driveway bodes well
On this drizzly day in the middle of February.

A SNOWMAN NAMED STORY

So this morning, I set out to write a story.
But my mind was weary, and
Great ponderous thoughts intervened.
It was snowing heavily outside my little window.
Great, ponderous flakes.
Why do I even write, I thought?
What is the point.?
And then it struck me!
Perfect snow—for IT—
Go out and build a snowman.
So I did.
And it melted in the afternoon sun.
Afterwards, I wrote my story.
And it will melt, too.
But I was happy.
I named my snowman Story.
And this is the story I wrote.

CRESCIT EUNDO

Gawd... am I the only one,
Who ever had to read
This old Roman philosopher Lucretius?
That's Titus Lucretius Carus.
Something he wrote called
De Rerum Natura about
The Nature of the Universe?
He was talking about thunder,
How it rumbles and rolls through the heavens.
Crescit Eundo, he wrote,
It grows as it goes.
What I wrote at the time,
On the cover of my notebook
Was:
Latin is a language as dead as it could be,
It killed the ancient Romans, and now it's killing me.
Years later,
Strolling through Old Town in Albuquerque,
I saw, scrolled on the flag of New Mexico
The motto chosen for the State,
The words: Crescit Eundo.
That Lucretius, I thought,
He sure had a way with the words,
A way to rumble and roll through the ages.

SOMEONE LOVES ME

Oh what a lonely summer that was.
Between jobs,
Between relationships,
Housesitting a drafty old place
In a seaside village in Maine.
Living alone, "recovering" as it was,
From whatever.
I'm not sure anyone
Even knew where I was.
Evenings were special.
Long walks through the village
Watching boats tie up at their moorings
Watching night fall over the harbor,
Avoiding contact with strangers,
Stopping every now and then,
At the village phone booth
And calling the number
Of the house I was tending.
Later, returning to the house after dark,
My spirits would lift at the sight
Of the little red blinky
On the answering machine.
Someone loved me!
Listening to my message,
I would thrill to the richness of the voice,
The kindness and wisdom
In the words that were spoken.
Years later,
On a day trip to that same seaside village
I will be chided by a granddaughter

About seatbelt protocol and safety.
She is so serious, and I love teasing her...
I will tell her about the blinky on my answering machine,
And I will concoct a long and silly story
About my sad and unhappy childhood
With no one to love me.
And now, I will tell her,
What you hear as an irritating buzzer,
Harping at me to buckle my seatbelt,
I hear as a soft voice,
Saying, *I love you, I love you,*
Please let me hold you and keep you safe.
With that, my granddaughter will look at me,
With this intense and quizzical look that she has.
But Grampy, she will say, ***I love you.***
And I will decide it's time
To stop making up silly stories,
To stop being silly altogether
And to stop for ice cream
At a little shop I know of
Just behind the spot
Where the old village phone booth
Had stood so alluringly
All those many years ago.

ABOUT ATMOSPHERE PRESS

Atmosphere Press is an independent, full-service publisher for excellent books in all genres and for all audiences. Learn more about what we do at atmospherepress.com.

We encourage you to check out some of Atmosphere's latest releases, which are available at Amazon.com and via order from your local bookstore:

Auroras Over Acadia, poetry by Paul Liebow

Rags to Rags, nonfiction by Ellie Guzman

Minnesota and Other Poems, poetry by Daniel N. Nelson

On a Lark, a novel by Sandra Fox Murphy

Ivory Tower, a novel by Grant Matthew Jenkins

Tailgater, short stories by Graham Guest

Plastic Jesus and Other Stories, short stories by Judith Ets-Hokin

The Quintessents, a novel by Clem Fiorentino

The Devil's in the Details, short stories by VA Christie

Heat in the Vegas Night, nonfiction by Jerry Reedy

Chimera in New Orleans, a novel by Lauren Savoie

The Neurosis of George Fairbanks, a novel by Jonathan Kumar

Blue Screen, a novel by Jim van de Erve

Young Yogi and the Mind Monsters, an illustrated retelling of Patanjali by Sonja Radvila

The Magpie and The Turtle, a picture book by Timothy Yeahquo

Come Kill Me!, short stories by Mackinley Greenlaw

The Unexpected Aneurysm of the Potato Blossom Queen, short stories by Garrett Socol

ABOUT THE AUTHOR

In 1971, Hans abandoned an academic career and moved to Maine. He and his family were part of what came to be known as the Homesteading Movement, inspired in part by the writings of Scott and Helen Nearing and the publication of something called *The Whole Earth Catalogue*. Hans and his family built their own house, raised two fine daughters along with dairy goats and organic vegetables, participated in the great statewide Common Ground Country Fair, and did their best to carve a niche for themselves in their community at large.

Throughout it all, Hans worked at various jobs – as a teacher, a newspaper reporter, a mason's tender, a sign-maker, a woodcarver, and a mentor among what he calls The Lost Children of Maine. He's been deeply involved in something called The Great Pond Mountain Conservation Trust in Orland, Maine, where he's run programs for children and serves as photographer for various events and meetings.

Hans has been a writer in one form or another all his life, including various stints as a newspaper reporter, and he's been represented in a number of small publications. At one point in his life, he earned advanced degrees in literature and linguistics, and he covered the State of Connecticut as a field worker for The Dictionary of American Regional English. Over the years in Maine, he's written a number of funny (he thinks) stories and accounts of what's been going on around him.

Currently, Hans lives with his partner, Nancy in Bucksport, Maine. He's built himself a little room upstairs in the barnlet attached to their house, and he views the world through the branches of a great oak tree just outside his window.